THE MAN
I NEVER KNEW

How Leadership Can Be Developed by Faith, Family, & Friends

SAMUEL L. JONES, Ph.D

Copyright © 2016 by Samuel L. Jones
All rights reserved. This book or any portion thereof
may not be reproduced or used in any manner whatsoever
without the express written permission of the publisher except
for the use of brief quotations in a book review.

Limits of Liability and Disclaimer of Warranty

The author and publisher shall not be liable for your misuse of this material. This book is strictly for informational and educational purposes. The purpose of this book is to educate and entertain. The author and/or publisher do not guarantee that anyone following these techniques, suggestions, tips, ideas, or strategies will become successful. The author and/or publisher shall have neither liability nor responsibility to anyone with respect to any loss or damage caused, or alleged to be caused, directly or indirectly by the information contained in this book.

Views expressed in this publication do not necessarily reflect the views of the publisher.

Printed in the United States of America

Cover Design: Studio 5 Agency

ISBN: 978-0692759394

KEEN VISION PUBLISHING, LLC

www.keen-vision.com

DEDICATION

This book is dedicated to my grandmother, *Melissa "Madea" Shelton* (1925-2004). This book is about the meaning of leadership and influence. I have learned that while it is important to have great influential people in my life, I can also be influential in the lives of others. Everything Madea did in life was to show joy, resolve, and commitment to whatever task was at hand. My fondest memory of her was when she would take me fishing. She was as happy as can be sitting on her bucket waiting for a fish to bite. I did not know it then, but that was one of the most precious gifts a grandparent could give. It was important for me to see her enjoying her time doing something she loved as she taught small, yet valuable lessons about life. My grandmother's integrity, humility, love, and compassion for people left an indelible impression on my life. I will be eternally grateful for her example.

To my wife, *Sarah*, the woman of my dreams and my best friend, I dedicate this book and my life to you. I am deeply thankful for my great fortune to be married to you. After sixteen years of marriage, you continue to inspire me to become a better man. You are not only my most helpful supporter; you are also my deepest and most enduring admirer for anything I aspire to do. Not only did you provide emotional support throughout the writing process, but you helped me arrive at many of the ideas reflected in this book. I believe this book would have only been a dream if you were not in my life. My ultimate definition of success is having a spouse who loves and respects you even more as the years go by. Needless to say, you are my queen, which makes me want to be your king.

ACKNOWLEDGEMENTS

To say this book is by "Samuel L. Jones" overstates the magnitude of its entire meaning. I have been blessed with many wonderful people who have made such an impact on my life. The thought of attempting to name them all is very intimidating. Without the significant contributions made by several people, this book would be inexistent. Many thanks to all who had a role in helping me complete this task whether it was through kindness, patience, hard work, or whispered prayers.

I want to express gratitude to my editor, *Jennifer Arndt*. At each stage of the editorial process for each chapter, you have been insightful, meticulous, and tenacious in your enthusiasm for this project. I believe you understood what I was trying to accomplish with the book before I did, and you gently but firmly brought me into line whenever I strayed from my own voice. Thank you for the sacrifice you made with your family to complete this project.

To my basketball coach at West Bolivar High School in Rosedale, Mississippi, *Willie E. Thomas*. Thank you for seeing something in me way before I would believe it of myself. You have been a constant example of what a man should be. More than you will ever know, I've always appreciated your honesty and the open challenges you placed before me. Your impact in my life will always be present.

I want to thank my mother, *Girte Jones*. Even though we haven't always agreed on everything in life, it's always good to know that I can always hear you say I love you. I also want to thank my parents-in-law, *Dorothy and MC Clark*. Even though the law says that I married into your family, the love, support, and encouragement you've given me has made me feel as if I was born into the family. I appreciate you all for being God-fearing people. You will always have an impact on my life because I see you as parents.

And last but not least, I want to thank my spiritual leader and pastor, *Reverend Walter L. Moore*. Your Godly insight, inspiring sermons and friendship has continually fueled my desire to be a God-fearing man. Thank you for your continued support of my mission in life.

ABOUT THE AUTHOR

Professional Speaker. Author. Educator.

To whom much is given, much is required. This saying outlines the life and ongoing legacy of Dr. Samuel Jones. A proud native of Gunnison, MS, Dr. Jones is known as a passionate facilitator, motivational speaker and leadership development trainer who possesses the ability to connect with his audience on the topics that matter most. As a former college and professional athlete, he has acquired years of executive management experience. He has humbly overcame unbelievable obstacles to enjoy a life of service today. His most treasured accomplishment is his marriage to the former Sarah Clark of Richton, MS.

Dr. Jones is an ordained Minister and serves as the Superintendent of Sunday school at Peace and Goodwill Missionary Baptist Church in Richton, MS. He is the current owner of Life Changing Presentations, a seminars & presentations company that focuses on leadership development training, executive coaching, and strategic planning. He is also the Vice President of Student Affairs at Jones County Junior College in Ellisville, Mississippi and the leadership facilitator for the Mississippi Economic Council's Leadership Program.

Dr. Jones received a Bachelor's degree in Advertising and a Master's degree in Public Relations from the University of Southern Mississippi. He later continued his education at Mississippi State University where he received a Ph.D. in Educational Leadership. After his basketball career at USM, he continued his professional basketball career in Finland. He's conducted training and seminars for organizations such as General Electric Aviation, the Leadership MS program (sponsored by MEC), Farm Bureau, Entergy Inc., the USM Alumni Association, Mississippi State University, Navigator Credit Union, MS Power, and the MS Dept. of Education to name a few. He's a proud member of the National Speakers Association and a member of the Alumni Hall of Fame at the University of Southern Mississippi.

Today, he is passionate about success—the success of individuals and organizations. He shares his personal expertise through his experiences to highlight personal and professional know-hows that will indeed make a difference. He is the author of The Man I Never Knew: How Leadership Can Be Developed by Faith, Family, and Friends and Live Life on Purpose: From Discovery to Practice. His third book, Winning Before & Beyond the Finish Line: From Success to Significance will be released in the near future.

Contents

ACKNOWLEDGEMENTS vii
ABOUT THE AUTHOR ix
PREFACE 1

CHAPTER 1
EXPOSURE LEADS TO EXPERIENCE 5

CHAPTER 2
LEARNING TO LEAD AS OTHERS LAUGH 21

CHAPTER 3
THE TRUTH IS THE TRUTH 29

CHAPTER 4
SUCCESS BY DESIGN, NOT BY CHANCE 49

CHAPTER 5
CHANGE IS SCARY, BUT IT'S GOOD! 65

CHAPTER 6
OK! MEANS OPPORTUNITY KNOCKING 77

CHAPTER 7
THE MAKING OF A CHAMPION: FROM INSPIRATION TO APPLICATION 89

CHAPTER 8
YOUR TIPPING POINT IS YOUR NEXT STEP 101

CHAPTER 9
IT NEVER GETS EASIER, YOU JUST GET STRONGER 121

CHAPTER 10
THE ENDURING LEGACY 133

CHAPTER 11
THE MAN I KNOW NOW 147

WORKS CITED..165
NOTES..167

PREFACE

Colin Powell once said, "With some people, you spend an evening and with others you invest it. So be careful where you stop to inquire for directions along the road of life because you can end up following people who are not going anywhere." I was always told never to receive counsel from unproductive people or discuss my problems with someone incapable of contributing to the solution because those who never succeed are always first to give advice. You are certain to get the worst of the bargain when you exchange ideas with people who normally look out for themselves.

Growing up in the Mississippi Delta, I didn't always have the great idea of pursuing an education and changing my life because I had friends who wanted me to do the things they did, like hang out on the street corner or drink alcohol. I eventually tried their recreation, but never felt comfortable with my choices. That's when I realized that I was not cut out for that particular lifestyle. Not to mention, my grandmother, "Madea," definitely did not approve of me pursuing that way of life.

I always sensed there was some kind of mystic cosmic order of things, but I could not figure out how it all applied to my life. There were times when I felt like a foreigner in a strange land. I felt like I didn't fit in. I didn't think the way my friends thought during that time. It seemed as if I always had hope even though my friends didn't seem as hopeful. It appeared as though everyone else knew the whole story except me. I didn't want to ask questions because that would tell everyone else that I didn't know the answers. By the time I was twelve, I realized that my cohorts were in the same boat of confusion as me. I was just the only one to admit that I didn't have any answers to life's great questions. This is when I really began to think about who I wanted to be. I don't think those were my exact words, but I believe that's what I wondered. As I continued to ponder, my grandmother encouraged me to participate more in church events such as Sunday school. Even though I made fun of the church Deacons, I would help them start services on Sunday mornings and Wednesday evenings. My grandmother even taught me how to help the elderly in the church community by volunteering my time. I believe Madea knew I was anxious to get involved in some activities to fill that void in my life. My participation in athletics later in life also taught me some valuable lessons.

Colin Powell also said "wise is the person who fortifies his life with the right friendships and learns from each relationship. If you run with wolves, you will learn how to howl. But, if you associate with eagles, you will learn how to soar to great heights." So as you read this book, read it as if I were a friend, or your most trusted confidant, writing to you—and you alone to share all that I've learned up to this point. I encourage you to read it again and again. As you refresh your understanding of the lessons shared from each story, underline quotations, sentences and words that strike a chord with you. Memorize the principles that I share. Take the time to reflect on the questions at the end of each chapter. Each time that you read this book, you will see what lies behind each chapter and the person you never knew will be revealed. For through the words shared in this book, you will continue to evolve as a person, as a husband, as a wife, as a mother, as a father, as a sister, as a brother, as a mentor, as a mentee, as a leader, and as a servant.

I'm hoping that after you read *The Man I Never Knew*, you will agree that you need people in your life to influence you the way I did. More importantly, I pray that you'll discover the 'Person' you never knew. This book was written with an open heart, physically, spiritually, and emotionally, and I hope that you will read it the same way. Don't wait to start reading! The world can no longer wait to meet that person we never knew…and that person is YOU!

Samuel L. Jones
Ellisville, MS

CHAPTER 1

EXPOSURE LEADS TO EXPERIENCE

To be conscious that you are ignorant of the facts is a great step to knowledge.

—*Benjamin Disraeli*

It's December 8, 2006, about 9:45 p.m., a cold Friday night, and we are driving south on Highway 45 from Mississippi State University in Starkville headed back to the big ol' town of Ellisville, Mississippi. In the truck with me are my wife, Sarah; my mother-in-law, Dorothy Clark; and my father-in-law, MC Clark. We are headed back home after my graduation from MSU with my doctorate in educational leadership. This Ph.D. is something that I had been working toward for three years, and now it has finally come to pass. During this ride back while everyone else in the truck is asleep, I have time to reflect on this accomplishment, and I can remember where I came from and what I had to endure to reach this goal. To put it all into perspective, I was just a country boy from the Mississippi Delta who had just earned his doctorate. As the tears flow from my eyes, I am encouraged by my recollection to tell my story to motivate others on their journey.

To better understand how I got here, let's go back to where my story began in the Mississippi Delta. The first thing to know about the Mississippi Delta is that it isn't really a delta. The Mississippi River Delta, the mouth of the Mississippi, is actually about three hundred miles south of where I grew up. The Mississippi Delta lies between the Mississippi and Yazoo rivers. When I was a small boy, there were fields of crops as far as the eye could see. Every direction I looked, I would see flat, dusty fields. Looking back on that now as an adult, it's apparent that agriculture had long been the backbone of the local economy with hundreds of thousands of acres of cotton, rice, and soybeans. In my view, no other area of the country better represents the South than the Mississippi Delta.

Luther Brown, the associate dean for Delta Regional Development and director of the Delta Center for Culture and Learning at Delta State University, painted a picture of the Delta when he wrote:

The Man I Never Knew   Samuel L. Jones, Ph.D.

The Mississippi Delta stretches like a sun-ripened raisin across the flatlands of northwest Mississippi, and has been a slow way of life for decades. The birthplace of the blues and home to some of the richest agricultural land in the United States, the predominantly African-American region is bleeding dry as the tax base shrivels and people leave in search of work.

That is a pretty accurate description of the Delta on the surface. The Delta was hit hard by the economy downturn in 2008 only it began in the Delta long before the nation felt the crisis. For a stranger driving through the Delta now, it could easily seem like a forgotten land in America because of the dilapidated cotton mills, the boarded-up storefronts and the open fields with shotgun houses lined up row after row. Found in most southern states, shotgun houses are small, narrow houses consisting of three to five rooms in a row with no hallways. According to Shotgun House: An African Architectural Legacy, as referenced on Wikipedia, the term "shotgun house" was common after about 1940 and is said to come from the saying that someone could fire a shotgun through the front door, and the pellets would fly cleanly through the house and out the back door.

The life in the Delta is not all bleak. Some well-known people have come from this area. Jim Henson, creator of the Muppets, is from Leland. Actor James Earl Jones is from Arkabutla. Television personality Oprah Winfrey is from Kosciusko. Former quarterback Archie Manning is from Drew. Singer and songwriter Sam Cooke is from Clarksdale. As you can see, some pretty prominent people came from the Delta, so that is why I see hope and inspiration every time I go back to visit family members and friends. When I go back to the Delta, I always leave inspired and proud to know that this place helped mold me to be the person I am today. I know that my passion for life, my drive to succeed, and my hope for tomorrow all started on the dusty playgrounds of the Mississippi Delta. When I reflect back on my childhood, I can still smell the cotton when it's ready to be processed, and I can hear the cotton gins working all night. I can feel the heat of the long, hot summer days. The Mississippi Delta is a very special place to me, and it always will be.

The Mississippi Delta is a very unique place. People from all over the world travel thousands of miles to sample this remarkable region. I'm always proud to go back to see what's changed and what thankfully hasn't about this authentic slice of America.

Growing up there, I lived with my grandmother, Melissa Shelton. She raised me as my mother attended Jackson State University in Jackson, Mississippi. Everybody in the family called my grandmother "Madea" from the time I was a young boy. She was the original Madea, way before Tyler Perry's character. She was a very stern person who said what she meant and meant what she said. She was always concerned with me doing my best. She always said

The Man I Never Knew

Samuel L. Jones, Ph.D.

to me, "Sam, if you're going to be a garbage man on the garbage truck, be the best garbage man there ever was. Always know that you're signing your name to your work. Make sure you're always proud to represent your work." She believed in doing things right and doing things to the best of her ability. It was important to her that I also learned to do so. Madea did not have a formal education, but she was wise beyond her years.

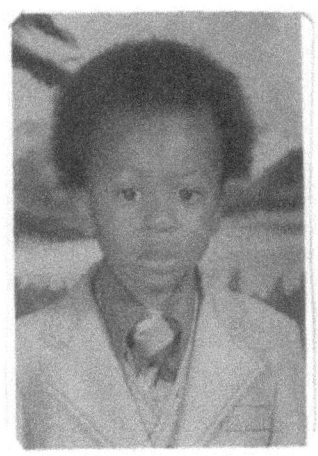

Here's me at age four. I've always had a knack for wearing suits and ties.

I can remember when I was about seven or eight years old, and I would follow her around wherever she went. If she went somewhere and I didn't get a chance to go, it felt like someone pierced my heart with a knife and twisted it. That's how much I wanted to be around her. Just to be in her company was enough for me because she was always giving wisdom in terms of helping me learn how to live. Even as a young boy, that really made an impression on me. For example, many times she would take me fishing with her. Adults during that time would fish all day long, from sun up to sun down. This was a very special lesson for me. During those long, hot summer days in the Delta, I hated fishing all day with a passion, but it was okay because I was with Madea. When we were fishing, as long as the fish were biting I was happy to be there, but as soon as they stopped biting, I was ready to pack up and leave. Madea would always have a lesson in whatever we were doing. Her lesson in this fishing phase was to always BE PATIENT! Of course, a seven or eight-year-old boy couldn't even spell patience, at least I couldn't. Eventually, I got to the point where I could go fishing with her and not worry about catching anything. I believe that's when my patience began to grow. Today, some twenty-five or so years later, my favorite recreational sport/leisure activity is fishing. I don't think that is a coincidence.

As I mentioned before, my grandmother was very loving and kind, and she was very inspirational. Even though she did not have a formal education, she was able to teach me and others the best way she knew how because of her Godly wisdom. She would say things that would make us think, even though we didn't necessarily understand her meaning at the moment. For example, if someone liked to talk even without being familiar with the topic at hand, she would say, "You know, an empty wagon makes a lot of noise." That was her way of saying be cautious of sounding uninformed and not doing so much talking. She always taught me to use my words wisely because people would listen to what I said. Not only that, but people would form opinions about me based on the knowledge I might claim to have. Early on, I heard a lot of those sayings so I could learn their valuable lessons.

The Man I Never Knew   Samuel L. Jones, Ph.D.

I was fortunate that I had someone around like my grandmother to discipline me when I needed it the most and to encourage and celebrate me when I accomplished something. I don't think people get enough discipline and encouragement today. Of course, discipline helps you learn from your mistakes, and I don't think enough people understand that everyone needs discipline. Aristotle said, "We are what we repeatedly do. Excellence, then, is not an act, but a habit." My grandmother wanted me to recognize my mistakes and learn to overcome them. She wanted me to develop an attitude and spirit of excellence in everything that I do. I have no doubt that this is where my drive to succeed first originated.

Madea would also find creative ways to encourage and celebrate me even after I made a mistake. I can remember a specific example from a time when we went fishing when I was a little boy. I would play with the crickets we used for bait. I would get one cricket out of the can and let it hop around, and then I would catch it to put back in the can. Well, this particular day, the crickets seemed to be a little more hyper than usual, and I didn't pay attention to the details. As I released one cricket, I began to chase it down. I didn't pay attention to what I was doing. I left the lid off the can, and all the other crickets got out. Madea was so mad at me that I wanted to jump in the lake, and I didn't even know how to swim. I just knew I was going to get a spanking for losing all of her crickets. Of course, this incident interrupted her fishing time, but it didn't stop her from giving me a life lesson. She sat me down and explained to me that I needed to look at the details of what I was doing. She shared a few more things, but I don't think they all stayed with me. That was the encouragement part of her conversation with me. The discipline piece, on the other hand, was that I had to dig her some bait (the earthworms we fished with) because I lost all of her crickets. "Digging baits" is what we did to get earthworms. I had to get the shovel and dig up earthworms for her because of my carelessness. Thinking about this now, I realized that she was showing me kindness, grace, and mercy by not spanking me for losing her crickets. I learned my lesson that day, and I have not forgotten. Even today, I try to pay attention to details, and I still know how to dig baits.

My grandmother also encouraged and celebrated me through basketball, among other things. She always wanted me to be involved in sports and activities and to do my best. I was always a nervous and shy young man, but she wanted me to trust my coach. Coach Willie Earl Thomas saw my skills when I was in the seventh grade. I think he always knew I had great potential, and he wanted to expose me to new opportunities. I can remember when I was in the ninth grade, I was playing basketball, and Coach Thomas took the team to a basketball camp at the University of South Alabama in Mobile. I can vividly remember driving through Hattiesburg on Highway 49 and passing by the campus of the University of Southern Mississippi. My first thought was, "I want to go to school there." Keep in mind that this was a young man from the Delta, who was a five-hour drive away from home. College was a long time off, and I had no real plans to go, but the campus was so impressive that it made an indelible mark on me.

Upon returning home after the camp, I could tell Coach Thomas saw something in me that said, "I can do anything I want to do if I put my mind to it." He continued to push me harder than any of my teammates. Over the next couple of years, my basketball skills began to improve, and I began to be noticed by several college basketball recruiters. Those colleges included Delta State University in Cleveland, Mississippi; the University of North Texas in Denton, Texas; and the University of Southern Mississippi in Hattiesburg. Before beginning my senior year of high school, I had always said that I was never going to go to college. Much to my surprise at the time, being noticed by basketball recruiters was the beginning of all of my very important educational experiences, and it all started because of basketball.

During my senior year in high school, I had the pleasure of making my official visits to each of the schools I mentioned. Going on these recruiting visits to these schools in 1991, I was the first person in our family ever to fly on an airplane. That was the beginning of many firsts for our family. But there was one very weird visit that helped me decide which school to attend.

My first official visit was to the University of North Texas. My flight was out of Memphis, Tennessee, which was a two-hour drive from home. Even though this would be my first time to fly, I was really afraid, but we didn't have any problems at all. The flight was smooth sailing, but that's when I learned about "ear popping." Before that flight, I had no idea what that meant. After getting back home from that visit, it seemed it took a week for my ears to get back to normal. Also, I thought that all airports were like the ones in Memphis and Dallas. I would soon be surprised.

My flying experience really began to get interesting on my next flight, which was from Cleveland, MS to Hattiesburg, MS. I would soon learn that there is a big difference between flying from Memphis and flying from Cleveland. My grandmother and I lived about twenty minutes from Cleveland. Ralph Moore and Robert McInnis (assistant coaches at USM at the time) flew into the small airport at Delta State University to pick me up. At the time, I didn't realize how different this airport was, until I noticed the small plane that we would board to fly to Hattiesburg. Upon boarding the plane, we realized the plane would not start. Of course, I was trying to play it cool, calm, and collected since I had just flown the week before in a big plane to Dallas. But my nervousness began to show immediately when, within five minutes, an airport maintenance worker rolled out a cart with a battery jumper pack to start the plane. At first, I was thinking, "It looks like they've done this before." My second thought was, "What if the plane goes dead in the air?" I was no longer cool, calm, and collected. I was thinking, "This is really crazy." However, without further hesitation, the plane was started, and an hour and a half later, we landed at Camp Shelby, a military base just south of Hattiesburg.

During my recruiting visit, I stayed with Clarence Weatherspoon who was a senior basketball player at USM. Clarence went on to play several seasons in the NBA, and he is still a friend of mine today. Clarence and some other players had a night of partying all set up just for the recruits. And I was ready, willing, and able to enjoy myself, right? Wrong! I was actually back at the dorm sick with the flu.

After making it home from that visit, it was apparent that I needed to keep that experience in mind and trust that USM was the place for me to pursue my college education. The experience I'm talking about is the struggle to be successful. On my flight to Dallas, it seemed everything went as planned. We didn't have a single problem, and that was sort of scary. I was very used to overcoming obstacles to be successful. The trip to Dallas didn't teach me much, and the school was not a perfect fit for me. But the trip to Hattiesburg taught me several things, and it was a perfect fit because of the experience I had. First, jump-starting an airplane with a battery cable, that's unheard of. I had to learn how to trust that the professionals knew what they're doing. I don't think people believe me when I tell that story. Second, coming down with the flu during the visit was a crazy experience. But this showed me how compassionate everyone was. They cared for me during a time when they could have been enjoying themselves. Talk about obstacles! It was apparent I had to overcome several things on that trip. Those experiences and the caring attitudes of the players, coaches and the basketball community helped me choose USM. I'm glad I made that decision because I was able to graduate with a bachelor's degree in advertising.

To summarize all of this: First, my grandmother knew I needed a positive male figure during a crucial time in my life. I was looking for guidance from a male figure I needed at the time to stay out of trouble. Second, being exposed to different people, experiences and opportunities gave me other dreams and aspirations I never believed possible. The trip to the University of South Alabama for basketball camp changed my perspective on my life and opportunities available. It gave me the desire to spread my wings and fly. Lastly, I had to learn to trust my own life experiences. Each step along the way, it challenged me to be motivational, and it encouraged me to be successful. I had always thought it easy to get motivated and encouraged by someone else's life, but what about my own experiences? I'm hoping my experiences will help you learn from yours, and then you will share those experiences to help others.

This is the story of how I recognized the man I never knew. I believe we all have inspiring experiences to share. My grandmother was inspirational to me in so many ways that I can't count them all. I feel that my grandmother still has an impact on my life today. She passed away in 2004, but I can still hear her soft voice when I feel like I am dragging through the day. Madea taught me how to fish and how to produce patience, and she also taught me that I could do anything I set my mind to.

Today, I am an ordained minister, a motivational speaker, and the vice president of student affairs at Jones County Junior College in Ellisville, MS. These various roles have allowed me to position myself as a leader, not only on campus, but in my community. I have been able to network and serve others through various avenues and it's given me a tremendous platform to express my faith and share the leadership lessons I've learned over the years. I'm currently involved in volunteer projects through mentoring and also by serving on several community boards. These opportunities have allowed me to grow as a person and as a professional. I've also attended several conferences and workshops on leadership, and I've completed several leadership programs. Those experiences led to speaking engagements during which I talked to audiences about leadership, and I've always shared portions of my story. It eventually led me to become a professional motivation speaker, and it prepared me to accept my call into the ministry. Then it dawned on me. Not only do I need to continue to grow as a leader, but I need to tell more of my story so others can learn from me just as I have learned from the stories of others. This book is another way for me to share my platform. I'm also hoping this book inspires you to examine your life story and to be encouraged by the inspirational people in your life. If you think you don't have inspirational people around you, think again. As you explore the fascinating people in my life, I hope you can look around and find them in your life, too.

Complete the Chapter Review below. Record and date your responses in a journal or composition notebook.

CHAPTER REVIEW

1. What personal/professional experience has caused you to re-evaluate your priorities in personal or professional aspirations?

2. Based on the priorities you mentioned above, what are some other ways you can make a greater impact in your home, family, and community?

3. What resources (financial, network/connections, education) would you need to produce your desired impact? Are you willing to seek assistance from a mentor or a life/business coach?

4. Can you identify any other areas of awareness from reading Chapter One?

CHAPTER 2

LEARNING TO LEAD AS OTHERS LAUGH

Nothing shows a man's character more than what he laughs at.
—Author Unknown

I haven't always been the kind of man who could laugh at himself, especially when others are laughing at me. But I have one story related to my basketball career that changed my life and allowed me to focus and trust in my own leadership abilities. I'm thankful that I'm able to share this story now because I've learned to discover things about my leadership skills, whether good or bad, and these skills have helped me to have compassion for myself first, and then for others. I hope this story can do the same for you.

It's November 1992, and it's the first exhibition game of

the new college basketball season in my freshman year at the University of Southern Mississippi. And Midnight Madness was just a few nights ago. (Midnight Madness is an annual event in mid-October on college campuses that celebrates the first day that the NCAA permits formal basketball practices.) And this exhibition game is my first official scrimmage with my new teammates. We line up on the court to scrimmage against a European travel team. Games like this do not count against our overall record, but this is an important game for me because it is my first college-level game. As the crowd is cheering and

This shot was taken my freshman year at the University of Southern Mississippi in 1992. Can you say baby face?

going wild, I can feel the nervousness and excitement in the pit of my stomach as if it's tied in a knot. The referee throws up the jump ball. My teammate Glen Whisby tips it to me. I get the ball, and I dribble it behind my back, between my legs as I drive towards the basket. I explode off the floor seemingly from the free throw line. As I'm flying towards the basket, I can hear the wind in my ears as if I'm flying among the clouds. The next thing I hear is, "Whoosh!!!" Slam dunk with two hands. All of a sudden, silence! It seems as if I can hear crickets. What happened? I dunked . . . in the wrong goal.

It's not unusual in a basketball game to see someone scoring in the wrong basket by tipping it in or throwing the ball to the other team but dunking in the wrong basket? Even to this day, I can't believe that happened, but it did. But even in that, there is a lesson to be learned. Of course, my time at USM was a great experience, but dunking in the wrong goal almost ruined it. Despite the error, we won the game. As I reflect back on this scenario, I see my teammates and myself going out to half-court to shake hands just before the tip-off. Each team should have lined up facing the opposing bench for each half of the game. On this occasion, my teammate Glen Whisby, who played center, had lined up on the wrong side of the court. That was wrong because each team is charged with lining up on specific sides of the court to start the game. Both teams had actually lined up on the wrong side. And since I was the point guard, I had lined up directly opposite of Glen as normal. The play we had designed was for the ball to be tipped to me so I could score right away. As Glen tipped this ball to me, I immediately did as I always had in practice, and I scored the basket. I jumped as high as I could, and I dunked the basketball as hard as I could. After I scored, it was pure silence as I landed with joy and excitement. At the time, I did not know that silence could be so loud. After about fifteen seconds had passed, even though it seemed like five minutes, both my team and the crowd laughed because they realized what had just happened.

That was a moment I will never forget. Of course, my teammates gave me a very hard time about dunking in the wrong net. However, until I was able to laugh about it, I didn't learn to deal with the embarrassment and not let it continue to affect me. I tell this story, and I continue to laugh about it because I think it humanizes me for a couple of reasons. First, I never want to be the kind of person that takes himself too seriously. I want people to know that I'm not perfect and that I can laugh at myself. I want people to know that I can handle difficulties with firmness and humility. My grandmother always said, "If you can't stand the heat, get out of the kitchen. Always know that the kitchen might be hot, but it'll eventually cool off so hang in there." I needed her words during a time such as that, being an eighteen-year-old freshmen basketball player and making such a big mistake as dunking in the wrong goal. Secondly, I share this experience because I want my readers to understand the lesson from this mistake. I didn't take my leadership position seriously enough at the time. As the point guard, my job was to be sure everyone was in the correct position before the game started. I allowed my center to line up on the wrong side of the court, and I followed his lead. I should have recognized the error and corrected myself first then my teammates. I was excited to be on the court, but I didn't pay attention to the details. I had forgotten the cricket lesson with my grandmother on the banks of the pond. I realized that it's OK to be excited about what you are doing, but it's important to focus on the specific details of the job at hand.

And, of course, I was embarrassed because I let my mind focus on how bad this situation was at the time. For me to get beyond this situation, I had to realize that this was an important opportunity to learn from. As an eighteen-year-old, it's easy to focus on the negative, but it's much harder to identify something positive from an experience that's uncomfortable and embarrassing, like dunking in the wrong goal. In the end, it took some time for me feel comfortable with the fact that it was not life or death and that this situation would get better. I had to remove the distraction of embarrassment to realize that life was not over. I had to make it a goal to laugh and smile every time I heard someone talk about the incident. It was hard for me to do at first, but it got easier and easier. I believe the younger you are, the more likely you will give attention to many unimportant things. I feel I was still getting to know my personal strengths and weaknesses. I learned that if I focus my thinking on only negative things, then my aspirations will change, and I will waste time and energy as life passes me by. As I've gotten older and had new and varied experiences, I understand the need to focus on positive things in my life, and I know positive thinking fuels my aspirations.

Today, I share that experience with audiences so they can not only laugh at the scenario but learn some valuable leadership lessons from my mistake. Richard Bach, a motivational writer, writes, "There are no mistakes. The events we bring upon ourselves, no matter how unpleasant, are necessary to learn what we need to learn; whatever steps we take, they're necessary to reach the places we've chosen to go." I had to take personal responsibility for my actions, learn from them, and laugh at them to inspire others. I think this is one of the first events where I had to examine my leadership skills and eventually act on them. I now realize this event was important in my life because it taught me how to laugh at my mistakes and it humanizes me if others put me on a pedestal. I also believe this experience of embarrassing myself continues to keep me humble. So as you laugh at this event, I will laugh with you as I continue

One of my many dunks at USM. This one, however, was in the correct goal.

to learn to lead. And as others laugh at you, be sure you also continue to laugh and lead with compassion. Quotation anthologist Terri Guillemets says don't cast a shadow on anyone unless you're providing shade. So whenever I make a mistake and others laugh, I have compassion for them as I laugh with them because I don't want to cast a shadow of anger or resentment on them because of my mistake. I want to provide a shade of humility and consideration for them by having confidence in who I am despite my mistake as I continue to learn how to lead.

Complete the Chapter Review below. Record and date your responses in a journal or composition notebook.

CHAPTER REVIEW

1. What has been one of the biggest mistakes you've made in front of 10 or more people?

2. What leadership lesson can you share from that mistake?

3. Are you embarrassed to share it with the people you're leading? If so, why?

CHAPTER 3

THE TRUTH IS THE TRUTH

What you perceive, your observations, feelings, interpretations, are all your truth. Your truth is important. Yet it is not The Truth.
—Linda Ellinor

In the award-winning film Chariots of Fire, one of the main characters is legendary British sprinter Harold Abrahams, who will sacrifice anything to achieve his goal -- except his honor. Chariots of Fire is a passionate, heartwarming story of two men who run, not to compete, but to prove something to the world.

Harold is obsessed with winning, but in a preliminary 100-meter race leading up to the 1924 Olympics, he is soundly beaten by his rival, Eric Liddell. Harold's response is deep despair and frustration because he had worked so hard. When his girlfriend Sybil tries to encourage him, Harold angrily declares, "I run to win. If I can't win, I won't run!" Sybil responds wisely, "If you don't run, you can't win." This film is a perfect illustration of how I had to accept the truth by learning to sacrifice things to become a winner and achieve goals for a bigger purpose.

In August 1997, after graduating from the University of Southern Mississippi with a bachelor of arts in advertising, I began to focus my dreams and aspirations on playing professional basketball. Of course playing professionally is the goal of most college athletes. Deep in my heart and mind, I knew that I should be pursuing other things, like furthering my education and/or working but I didn't think that I was ready to take on that role. One thing I learned is that life will teach you things you didn't plan for. My grandmother always told me that God will allow you to do what you want to do, but at the end of the day, you'll still have to depend on Him for everything and follow the will He has for your life. As you continue to read, you'll probably be as surprised as I was about what God had in store for me. I always knew my grandmother was right but I never really wanted to accept it. I had always wanted to keep the status quo, but since the truth is the truth, I learned that once I accept it as the truth, my life became less stressful because I didn't have to control everything.

Madea always told me to do my best and let the chips fall where they may because God has a plan for you life. In other words, shoot for the moon and if I only get to the stars, then it isn't a bad deal. So with that in mind, after graduation, I hired a professional agent with the hopes of getting a professional basketball contract with an NBA team or a European team. The first thing I needed to do was to create my personal basketball highlight film for prospective teams. At first, I did not know where to begin, but I had some friends in the radio/TV/film department at USM who helped me get that process started. My highlight tape was about four minutes long, and it showcased my basketball skills. It showed my ability to score in a variety of ways; it showed my dribbling and passing skills. It also showed my defensive skills. It was sort of a job interview without me saying a word. Once my tape was distributed, I was offered the opportunity to travel to the Nike headquarters in Beaverton, Oregon, for a professional basketball mini-camp. The mini-camp consisted of players pursuing professional basketball careers along with scouts from other professional leagues.

Most people don't realize that the average basketball player has a very slim chance of making it to the NBA or any other professional league. There are only sixty players taken in every NBA draft and even sometimes those drafted don't make the team. In college, just like high school, a player has to have great stats, size, and speed, athletic ability and have people notice him have a shot at making it to the pros. But with that being said, receiving a contract offer to play professional basketball is still a great success, even though it's in a foreign country.

Needless to say, I knew I only had a slim chance of making it to the NBA, but I wanted to give it a shot. In other words, it was a leap of faith of continuing my basketball career. Author, poet, and educator Patrick Overton said, "When you have come to the edge of all light that you know; and you are about to drop off into darkness of the unknown, faith is knowing one or two things will happen: There will be something solid to stand on, or you will be taught to fly." For me, the edge of all light that I knew was my professional basketball experience. I think I found both something to stand on, and I was taught to fly when I came to that edge of light, and I dropped off into the darkness of the unknown.

A month after my tape was sent out, my agent called and said I had an offer for a one-year contract to play in Finland. Now, as a young man who had grown up in the heart of the Mississippi Delta, I had no idea where Finland was located or which language was spoken there. I had to decide whether to take advantage of this opportunity to play professional basketball. Without hesitation, I signed the contract and started applying for the proper documentation, including a work visa for international travel, to prepare for the trip. In the midst of the excitement, I was very nervous and anxious because I would be the first person in my family to travel out of the country. I was a twenty-two-year-old young man who did not yet know how this experience would change the rest of

The Man I Never Knew   Samuel L. Jones, Ph.D.

his life. Before leaving the United States, I tried to prepare myself as best as I could for Finland. I found books that had interesting facts about the country. I tried to learn their language a bit but without much success. But I was able to learn some common words like hello, thank you, and good-bye.

Now with my conscious clear and ready for this new journey, I boarded the airplane in Jackson, Mississippi, with connecting flights to Atlanta and New York to Helsinki, Finland. I was hoping that at any point that the airport maintenance staff wouldn't have to roll a cart out to start the plane. All in all, my complete travel time was about eighteen hours including layovers, so it was a long day of travel. I arrived in Finland in mid-August with the temperature averaging about eighty degrees and each day averaged eighteen hours of sunlight. Those long days of sunshine were one of the craziest things for me to get used to. I would try to sleep at 10:00 p.m. and the sun would still be shining. Eventually, I got used to it. If not, it would have been a very, very long stay.

My new team consisted of players from Finland and two Americans, including me. The Americans were considered heroes coming to save the day. We played a twenty-two game season with the games on Saturdays and some Wednesdays. During my season there, I averaged seventeen points, five rebounds, and three assists. Looking back now, it was a good season. About two weeks before the end of the season, I believe that I had a life-changing event that I want to share. Normally after every game, all the American players would meet in Helsinki to party and hang out. There were two American players on each of the twelve teams in the league's three divisions, so there was always a large group of us meeting up. So after a long night of dancing and hanging out, I woke up at about 3 am with surprise and confusion, as if someone else was present in my bedroom.

I was normally very tired after we had played a game and been hanging out in Helsinki, but this was nothing like any other morning. As I was lying there, it seemed as if my world and everything in it had stopped. I remember just laying there in a calm and peaceful state. And then, I noticed a very calm, soft, smooth voice in the pit of my soul that whispered, "Son, you know you are supposed to be doing something else." And as I lay there, I can feel the chill bumps run all over my body. Immediately, I knew that it was the voice of God speaking to directly to me. I didn't know what to think or feel at the point.

This reminded me of the story in the Bible from 1 Kings about the prophet Elijah. Elijah had just won a tremendous victory over the prophets of Baal but was now wallowing in self-pity in a cave, and God was speaking to him:

The Man I Never Knew   Samuel L. Jones, Ph.D.

And behold, the Lord passed by, and a great and strong wind tore into the mountains and broke the rocks in pieces before the Lord, but the Lord was not in the wind; and after the wind and earthquake, but the Lord was not in the earthquake; and after the earthquake a fire, but the Lord was not in the fire; and after the fire a still small voice.

Like Elijah, I had just won a tremendous victory by overcoming all the odds of becoming a professional basketball player, but I was definitely in a cave. I was in a cave in my mind because I thought I was actually living my life's dream of playing professional basketball. My first reaction was, "God I heard your voice." Then I was thinking, "What should I do next? Or What do I do next?" I've learned to really try to understand God's will for my life now when I know that he is speaking to me. I believe this is the day my life's purpose began to be formulated.

Every time I tell that story, I can feel the hair rise on the back of my neck because of the truth and realness of it all. I believe God had always told me I should be doing something different when I said I wanted to play professional basketball, but I just never really wanted to listen. Have you been there done that? For me, I believe that playing professional basketball was one of those things he allowed me to do until I was ready to hear his voice. I guess it took me going to a strange foreign land to hear and act on the voice of God. That strange land was Finland. It took me several days to actually accept this call. I know I overanalyzed the decision to change career paths. I was struggling with my decisions. I kept thinking, "What do I do next? Do I finish the basketball season or do I go home and wait to see what's next?" I didn't have anyone in Finland nor anyone back home to help me to decide. After finally accepting this call, I then remembered that I always wanted to be thought of as more than just an athlete. My dreams and aspirations of being more than an athlete became more realistic at that point. I knew my next few decisions as to how to get this new journey started would take some real faith. Before this moment, faith was only something I heard my grandmother talk about, but this was an opportunity for me to live out what I believed. So at the end of that season, I thought my mind was made up about pursuing something other than basketball. On my flight home from Finland after the season, I was a little confused as to what my next steps would be because I was still somewhat focused on what I wanted. I thought I had found my faith and was ready to apply it to all my decisions. Unfortunately, I realized I wasn't ready, and my faith would take a backseat.

Arriving back home in America was a very exciting time for me. I had an opportunity to catch up on all the latest news and developments with family, friends, and others in the Delta that I hadn't seen during my time away. When all that excitement of being home was over, I still came back to the question, "What's next for me?" I eventually worked odd jobs here and there to keep from spending the money I had saved in Finland. As days turned into weeks, and weeks turned to months, I became very nervous and anxious because I felt like I was just wasting my time. I knew I needed to make some plans, so I decided that I would try to go back overseas to continue my professional basketball career. I still wasn't putting faith into action at this point. This was the fall of 1998, and I was eagerly awaiting a call from my agent to hear where my next professional stop would be. I got a call, but unfortunately, it was not the call I wanted to hear. The call I got on October 26, 1998, was that the NBA was on strike. My agent called me and said, "The NBA owners have forced a player lockout which led to the cancellation of the entire preseason and the first weeks of the regular

Action from my professional basketball days in Finland.

season." When I first heard the news, I thought, "Yes! Maybe I'll have a shot at staying in America to play." After the initial excitement, reality sunk in really quickly. I soon realized getting picked up by the NBA was not going to be a possibility. Also, other realities began to become clear. It was like a domino effect. I thought that an NBA strike would not have an effect on other leagues. Wrong! It had a major effect. Teams in the European leagues put their contract options on hold for players like me. They had hopes of possibly signing striking NBA players to play in their leagues. I soon realized that my basketball season, at least for the time being, would be put on hold. Looking back, I truly believed that this was one of the several events that would help me to strengthen my faith. During that experience, it was as if I didn't have any faith because I was going back on what God had told me and what I thought I had accepted which was to change career paths. I don't believe that I was trusting him like I should. The NBA season resumed some six or eight weeks later, and I was still lost as to what my next step should be—should I continue to attempt to resume my basketball career or choose another path? I worked several jobs here and there, including Mason's Plywood Company, Structure Clothing (known today as Express Men), United Parcel Service and Sunbeam Company.

During this time, I was still actively working out (running and lifting weights) and playing basketball to stay in shape

The Man I Never Knew   Samuel L. Jones, Ph.D.

while I was working these jobs. Looking back, that behavior (working out and playing basketball) showed that I still hadn't accepted the fact that I was right in the middle of preparing to change careers. I was still showing that my faith was weak because I wasn't trusting God like I needed to. My job at Sunbeam, with a twelve-hour shift beginning at seven o'clock in the morning, would change all of that. With that work schedule, I was actually working from sun up to sun down, and it was very frustrating and time-consuming for me. My job at Sunbeam was to screw on the lids for small containers from 7 am to 7 pm. I had to stand in one spot, look down, and screw on lids. This kind of work was very painful for my neck, my joints, and my fingertips. I do know this, because of this experience, I now have great respect and appreciation for blue-collar workers and those who work in factories. This is the point where I made a decision to get serious about my faith. You see, I need a serious dose of humility because this experience created an atmosphere that I would need to truly depend on God. Not just talk about it, but actually make decisions based on that principle. I prayed to God, "Lord, you know I'm your servant, I know I have not trusted you like I should, I know what you promised me, I know what your word says…but I'm now humble and ready to follow the will that you have for my life…I recognize that I need you to guide me in this thing called life. Lord, help me to find that thing that I'm supposed to be doing for you." And I believe this was the day that I created the atmosphere for the awareness of God's presence in my life and also when I actively began to live out my faith. Author and pastor Robert Schuller states, "Faith is no irresponsible shot in the dark. It is a responsible trust in God, who knows the desires of your hearts, the dreams you are given, and the goals you have set. He will always guide your paths right." That situation of working in a factory with a college degree humbled me and allowed me to trust more in not what I said or wanted for myself but to trust more in what God said and what he wanted for my life. I knew I had to trust God to change this situation and to change my life.

Two weeks later, after getting off work at Sunbeam, I arrived home to find a message on my answering machine. The message was from Coach Robert McInnis, one of my former assistant basketball coaches from the University of Southern Mississippi. He is better known as Coach Mac. I've always trusted Coach Mac because he was one of the coaches who recruited me while in high school. Of course, I really got to know him during my college career. We still laugh about the airplane trip from Cleveland. Coach Mac left a message on my answering machine that said, "Hey, Sam, this is Coach Mac, I would love for you to join me for lunch one day. I'm at Jones County Junior College now. Give me a call when you get a chance. Talk soon, bye." I knew he had just accepted the head coaching

The Man I Never Knew   Samuel L. Jones, Ph.D.

position at JCJC. After listening to that message, I had a gut feeling he was going to ask me to become his assistant basketball coach. Now my mind started to play tricks with me. First, I was thinking, what if he wants me to be his assistant, do I take it? But what if he doesn't want me to be his assistant, what do I do after that? On and on and on, my mind wondered and wondered. I finally decided to set up a lunch meeting with him to see what he had to say. And, you guessed it, he asked me to be his assistant basketball coach. Of course, I was always told never accept an offer the same day it's given because I should always take some time to think it over. So that night, I went home and put the pen to paper. I weighed my options by looking at salaries versus debts versus opportunities. Subsequently, I took less money than the other jobs I had previously worked to become Coach Mac's assistant. I decided that it was not about the money. I made a commitment to do something different that would allow me to give back to other basketball players. Even though I never had dreams of coaching but I did recognize that this would allow me to do something different. Then I started wondering, is this what God had in store for me all along? Once again, I was to be shocked and surprised by the answer.

During my first season as the assistant coach, we reached the state championship game and then the regional tournament finishing as runners-up in both. After that first year, I realized that being a basketball coaching was not for me, but I was not going to quit. I told myself, "I've never quit anything in my life, and I am not going to start now." There were plenty of times growing up in the Delta that I wanted to quit the activities I was participating in, but my grandmother would not allow me to. She had always told me that quitters never win, and winners never quit. She would also say that once you quit one thing, it becomes much easier to quit other things in life. So I really didn't have a choice in the matter of quitting coaching. I like what author Coleman Cox says about quitting, "Even the woodpecker owes his success to the fact that he uses his head and keeps pecking away until he finishes the job he starts." Needless to say, I would eventually start using my head, and I saw coaching through until the job was done.

I then started to pursue a master's degree in public relations while I continued to coach. This was also a great experience for me because I had always said that I was never going back to school. Have you ever said something that you would never do? For me, this wasn't the last time that statement would come back to haunt me. I just know that God knew the future because as soon as I finished my master's degree in 2002, I accepted an administrative position at Jones County Junior College. I became the assistant dean of student affairs part-time while I continued to coach basketball part time. My new job consisted of working with students in areas ranging from recruiting to disciplinary matters. Eventually, I became the assistant dean full time. I realized my job as a basketball coach was over when I had the opportunity to work in administration. In this position as the assistant dean, I had an epiphany of sorts. I figured since I was in administration, I needed to pursue my doctorate to have the opportunity for a promotion and growth. That statement, "I'm never going back to school," came up again. I immediately put it out of my mind, humbled myself and enrolled in the doctoral program at Mississippi State University in the summer of 2003.

When I first started the program, I had plenty of doubts about whether I could do the work. It's amazing how we doubt ourselves when we first start a new endeavor. And like everyone else in the program, I had another big concern, "What will I do my dissertation on?" A dissertation is a document submitted in support of a candidate for a degree or professional qualification presenting the author's research and findings to complete the doctorate. Each student is required to find a topic of interest, present a formal research proposal to a committee (normally three to five faculty members), and defend the final document. In my first class, the finance of community/junior colleges, I came up with my topic, "A Study of the Perceptions of Mississippi Legislators regarding the mission and goals of Mississippi Community and Junior Colleges." From that point, I used every class to conduct my informal research, and I learned as much as I could about this topic to convince my committee of its worthiness. That hard work and the help of others allowed me to finish the doctoral process in three years. Most universities give graduate students eight years to complete a doctorate program, but I was well pleased with how this turned out.

Looking back on it all now, I realize that getting my doctorate was never a goal of mine, but it was an opportunity God presented me with to show me the vision that he had for my life. This entire process went from me graduating college, to going overseas to play professional basketball, to coaching basketball, to earning a master's degree and to earning a doctorate. I've learned that it was never about me. It was all about me having the faith in following the plan God had for me. It was about going through situations in which I had to grow my faith to be in a position to help others find and have faith in something bigger than themselves.

I had always heard my grandmother talk about God, faith, religion and all those related spiritual concepts but they didn't always make sense to me. I was even the young man who always went to church and read the Bible. I always tried to do the right thing even when it seemed unpopular. But all those lessons I was taught never seemed real to me until I put them into practice in my own personal life. I don't think you will be indecisive if and when you know what your purpose is in life. Needless to say, my experiences have been reality checks for me. I've learned that while my calling may change my purpose will not. When I was in high school, my calling was to be the first in my family to get a scholarship to college. When I was in college, my calling was to lead myself and other athletes both on and off the playing field to do the right thing. When I was in Finland, my calling was to hear and respond in the correct manner to the voice of God. And of course now as an adult, my calling is to share my story and other inspirational stories with others and be an example of how the road to success is always under construction and that it's never a straight line. Have I always answered the call? No. But I believe God continues to give us chance after chance because of His love. I call it grace and mercy. I believe that sin is just missing the mark, not believing in God's power to help us overcome. So during the past ten years, my calling has changed, but my purpose has not. I believe my purpose is to trust and depend on God for everything I need, encourage people, motivate people and inspire people. And lastly, to spur people on in love. We have enough judgment in the world. We need more love.

That's why it is important not to do what you want to do if it does nothing for others. So I try to always keep Sybil's response in my heart and mind, "If you don't run, you can't win." That is the absolute truth, whether it is accepted or not. I'm just glad now that I try to accept the truth no matter who it comes from. I definitely try to accept the truth from God because I know with him, you can't lose.

Complete the Chapter Review below. Record and date your responses in a journal or composition notebook.

CHAPTER REVIEW

1. Identify something that you said that you would never do that you find yourself doing today?

2. What lessons can you share with others from the experience you shared in questions #1?

CHAPTER 4

SUCCESS BY DESIGN, NOT BY CHANCE

Success means having the courage, the determination, and the will to become the person you believe you were meant to be.

—George Sheehan

If you were to examine my personal life up to this point, you would guess that any success I've had would have been by chance. From graduating college, going overseas playing professional basketball, coaching, earning a master's degree, earning a doctorate, becoming an administrator at a college, and now writing this book, I've accomplished quite a few things. Some may think all those things happened by chance. I'm here to tell you that my accomplishments occurred by choice. It was hard to envision how I would achieve success growing up in the Delta, but I can honestly say now that it was by design all along because of hard work and the support that I received from others and my faith in God. I eventually learned that all success starts with the right kind of attitude.

Early in my basketball career in high school and college, I had a chance to play with and against some very talented players. I often heard my high school and college coaches say things like, "He looks like Tarzan, but he plays like Jane." During those days, I had no idea what that meant——because they weren't weak players by any mean——, but today I understand. The problem was that these very talented people had the look of successful basketball players, but they didn't have the mental attitudes of successful players. I've learned that people with bad attitudes can't be successful even if success is handed to them on a silver platter. Why not? Because people with negative attitudes often find fault even where there is none, so they eventually design failure. That is not by chance, it's by choice. As I've gotten older, I've learned the importance of two things: first, your attitude determines whether you succeed or fail in life; and second, you have to learn how to deal with people who need a complete attitude adjustment. For those reasons, whatever your attitude is, success is not by chance, it's by choice.

For example, look at some career leaders in two of my favorite sports, basketball and baseball. Sports are a great example of how your attitude shows what you truly believe. When you think of baseball, the most attractive and impressive statistic is the homerun, or I like to call it the "long ball." According to MLB.com, the top two all-time homerun leaders are Barry Bonds with 762 and Hank Aaron with 755. Those are remarkable numbers, but many people don't realize that they struck out a combined 2,922 times. Years later, Aaron was quoted as saying, "My motto was always to keep swinging. Whether I was in a slump or feeling badly or having trouble off the field, the only thing to do was keep swinging." I believe both men were successful because they had the cunning ability to choose their attitudes for success.

Living in Southern Mississippi, when I think of football, I can't help but think of Mississippian Brett Favre——an excellent example of someone with a great attitude who designed success based on this attitude. If nothing else, I believe Favre's career will be remembered for his record-setting achievements. According to Wikipedia, Favre holds the NFL career records for the following: all-time career leader in starts, all-time career leader in pass completions, all-time career leader in pass attempts, and all-time career leader in passing yards. Wikipedia also reports one record that stands out to me, the all-time career leader in passing touching downs in which Favre has 508 and Hall of Famer Dan Marino is in second place with 420. As you can see, that's a staggering difference. But most people don't know that Favre is also the all-time career leader in fumbles with 166 and the all-time career leader in thrown interceptions with 336. Favre has been quoted saying, "We're always trying to find ways to lower interceptions and stuff. My nature, I'm aggressive. I'll take shots, I'll take chances; therefore, you have mistakes," It looks like he has the right attitude to deal with success and failure.

Surely, these individuals: Barry Bonds, Hank Aaron, and Brett Favre had to have the right attitudes to face the situations they did and to come out winners. You can look at any group of successful people, and the common denominator will be their attitude. I've always thought if you want to change your attitude, you must change the way you think. So many times in life we take for granted the things we are already blessed with. We need to be encouraged no matter how bleak we think life looks and to always have a positive attitude. I try to always live by the ancient Persian saying, "I had the blues because I had no shoes until down the street, I met a man who had no feet."

In the fall of 2002, as the dean of student affairs, I had the pleasure of working with a student who was blind—a uniquely gifted young man. This student was unique because he had the cunning ability to share wisdom and insight based on simple physical things people with eyesight might take for granted. For the sake of this story, I'll call him Sherman. Sherman taught me a very important lesson about how success is by choice and that we all have special gifts, and we should use our gifts at all times to help other people. "Well," you might say, "how

The Man I Never Knew — Samuel L. Jones, Ph.D.

can a blind student help me?" There were actually two separate incidents with this student that I will remember for the rest of my life.

On one hot summer day, I noticed this young man walking across campus with his white folding walking cane. I noticed that he was doing this during the summer school break, a period between the spring and summer semester when classes were not in session. He walked persistently on campus even though he was not registered for school. I also noticed that he seemed serious and intent in what he was doing. On this day, I introduced myself and asked him if there was anything we at the college could do to help him. He gently said, "No, all is well." I thought to myself, "Surely, we can find some way to help him. What was this student doing walking around campus on a hot summer day when he wasn't a student yet? Why didn't he ask us to help him? Why did I bother to offer to help him if I knew I really couldn't?" I guess asking him if I could help is something I practice with anyone. I just wanted help in some small way. These were some of the questions I pondered to myself as I walked away.

Once the fall semester began, I started to get the answers to the questions I had the previous summer. I saw Sherman walking across the campus of Jones County Junior College once again; only this time, I noticed a confident, positive, and progressive walk. I spoke to him

Success by Design, Not by Chance

again and asked him how everything was going. He immediately said, "Everything is great. I know where all my classes are. I know where the library is. I know where the cafeteria is. I know where everything is on campus. Life is good." I was thinking, "Life is good! Wow! That's a great attitude to have when you can't see your way around." I once again gave him my name and asked him to let me know if we could help him in any way. When I got back to my office after that encounter with him, I thought to myself, "Why was life good to him from his point of view?" Then the answer hit me like a ton of bricks. An inspiring quote by former newscaster David Brinkley came to mind, "A successful man is one who can lay a firm foundation with the bricks others have thrown at him." Surely, most people judged Sherman from the standpoint that he is limited in what he can do because he is blind. I was guilty of that same misjudgment because I was assuming that he needed my help.

Sherman proved to me that no matter what problems you have, you don't have to be defeated. Instead of sitting around complaining that he was blind or that he didn't know his way around campus, Sherman spent the long, hot summer days training himself for the fall semester. He took advantage of the fact that the summer session had fewer than half the students of the rest of the year and positioned himself to be successful. His attitude showed that was positive about the college experience that he

The Man I Never Knew   Samuel L. Jones, Ph.D.

asked and answered the questions "How can I prepare myself for success at Jones County Junior College? What can I do to get comfortable with this school? What should I do this summer to help me pursue my education?" You know, we all can find reasons to stick to the status quo. Reasons that sound like, "Well, that's the best I can do! Well, nobody will help me! I don't have the talent that everyone else has!" Those are just a few of the excuses or reasons we use to talk ourselves out of preparing for success. That initial interaction with Sherman encouraged me to go beyond any obstacles I would ever face in my life.

You know, sometimes we assume people need our help. Most of the time, people just need our support and encouragement. I learned that by my experience with Sherman. I like the motivational tool that author, ex-coach and motivational speaker Lou Holtz uses. His method to "WIN" is to ask yourself What's Important Now? I think Sherman understood what was important then because he wanted to do all he could to be prepared to be a successful college student. Sherman's attitude encouraged me in my professional life. It showed me that no matter what accomplishments I might gain, there is always room to grow. I believe that where you are today is only a reflection of where you have been in your life, but it's not indicative of where you are going. This young man had been blind his entire life, yet he didn't let that stop him from what he was trying to accomplish. He understood that no matter what problems he was facing, he had to look beyond his circumstances. We have to have a vision from our hearts and minds and not just from our eyes. I believe Sherman is a perfect example of how to design successful attributes for your personal and professional life.

I later learned another important lesson from Sherman which was truly encouraging to me. A few semesters later, he began participating in the African-American Student Organization at Jones. This is where I learned quite a bit more about him and the gift that he had. Mr. Elbert Lewis, a former instructor at Jones, shared a story with me about his experience with Sherman. Mr. Lewis was taking a group of students to a conference in a school van. The other passengers asked Sherman to sit up front out of respect for him. Mr. Lewis shared with me two important facets of this experience that I believe are vital: our ability to be sincere and our ability to sense danger. As Mr. Lewis drove these students to their conference, Sherman shared something with him which he said he would never forget. Mr. Lewis asked this young man, "How are things going on campus?" Sherman began to share how everything was going. He talked about how he learned where everything was on campus and how he was getting around comfortably. I think Mr. Lewis was shocked because he thought this young man might complain, but he never did. Immediately, Sherman began to talk about how there are so many people on campus who try to help him because he's blind. Mr. Lewis instantly wanted to know how this young man knew that people wanted to help him, he couldn't see them! After a few pauses, Sherman said in a soft, inspiring voice, "Even though I can't see them; I can feel when people want to help me." Everyone in the van went silent! After a few seconds of pure silence, Mr. Lewis asked him to elaborate more in detail as to how he can feel when people want to help him. The example he gave was pretty much an everyday situation for him. He immediately said, "When I come to a building with my walking stick, people usually open the door for me. Not only can I feel their presence, but I can also feel their warmth and sincerity as they open the door for me. Not only that, I can feel when I'm walking on the sidewalks, and people gently step aside. There is something special about people being sincere." After hearing this, the other students in the van were shocked and surprised. After Mr. Lewis had heard all this, he was thinking about what was said, and he began to drift off the road while driving. Somehow, Mr. Lewis just continued to drift near the outside lane on the passenger side. Keep in mind, Sherman was riding in the front passenger seat of the van on this trip. If these students didn't believe Sherman before, they would believe him now! The next words out of Sherman's mouth were, "Mr. Lewis, I know I can't see but I would appreciate it if you would get me off the edge of this highway. I can feel that you have me close to this outside lane over here, and I don't want us to have an accident." Of course, when he said that, everyone laughed as if he had told the funniest joke in the world. After that, other students began to ask questions of Sherman to find out what other wisdom and knowledge he had. Sherman continued to share, and I think it made the other students realize that he's an ordinary person who can't see physically, but he could see spiritually, mentally, and emotionally. The biggest lesson he wanted them to learn is to be sincere in what they do because it can and will make a difference in the lives of people around them.

For me, I had always examined success based on physical standards, from financial to possessions to titles and so on. But as I write this book and reflect on my life and past experiences with students like Sherman, I've been encouraged to examine success from a mental, emotional and spiritual standpoint. I think as people we need to individualize our success to be effective to others. I try to take ownership of my attitude because that is what is needed to be committed. If you're committed, and something fails, then it hurts deeply. But if you never make the commitment and it fails, then you think it's not your fault, but you also won't be successful. But as you individualize your success, always remember that you have to take personal responsibility.

Over the years, I came up with four questions I considered to design success for my life. To be effective, you truly have to be honest with yourself. I'm glad I was honest with myself. I hope these questions can be relevant to your life as well.

Question 1: Are you a product of your environment?

If you are a product of your environment, you must become a product of your own design. In other words, you don't have to have the perfect environment growing up to be successful. I think people have to learn how to have dreams even though they live in a very tough environment. That's what I did in the Delta when I was a young boy. I dreamed of having a job where I would wear a suit and tie to work every day. I dreamed of traveling to places I had only heard of. I achieved my dream, and now I want to encourage other people to dream the unimaginable. If you dream the unimaginable, then you forget about your current environment. Once you forget about your environment, you eventually produce your own design. Needless to say, I don't want people to forget where they came from because their new design may be to go back to that original environment to facilitate change. In short, if you question whether or not you are all that you can be, now is the time to take a closer look as to why that is, and make the changes that need to be made. Don't blame your lack of success on your environment but know that it will be based on the expectations you place on yourself.

Success won't happen by itself, and no one else can do it for you. Decide the person you want to be, and then do whatever is necessary to be that person no matter what environment you are in.

Question 2: How important is your past to you?

Everyone has a past. I think you need to learn from the past, and then put it behind you. I believe the only things you should take from the past are warm memories of encouragement and the pain from lessons learned so that those choices will not be repeated. Everything else should stay where it is—in the past. Once you examine and learn from all of your past and present experiences, your past will then make you more capable of coping with fear, stress, and failure in the future because you will see your current success. Writer and clergyman Charles Swindoll says, "We cannot change our past. We cannot change the fact that people act in certain ways. We cannot change the inevitable. The only thing we can do is play on the one string we have, and that is our attitude." Every time I think about my past, I find strength, courage, and determination to take each step. When my past is mentioned in conversation or from the words in this book, I want people to see courage. It's easy to think of courage only in times of great danger or stress. But I've learned that courage is an everyday virtue to live life without regrets. We need the courage to seek the truth even when we know it may be painful. We need the courage to express our convictions when others challenge us. We need the courage to change when it's easier to remain comfortable. We need courage to learn and grow, especially when doing so exposes our weaknesses. And lastly, we need the courage to lead when being out front makes us an easy target for criticism. So, how important is success and your past to you? If it's really important, it will take courage to overcome your past to live in the present and step into a future of success. Comedian and actor Jonathan Winters says about success, "I couldn't wait for success . . . So I went ahead without it."

Question 3: Do you want to learn tomorrow?

I've learned that my real education started in school, but it would take the rest of my life to apply it. French poet, journalist, and novelist Anatole France wrote, "An education isn't how much you have committed to memory, or even how much you know. It's being able to differentiate between what you know and what you don't." In other words, never stop learning because learning fuels growth and growth is necessary for success. If you think about it, successful people and unsuccessful people view learning differently. Successful people crave knowledge by reading and by evaluating their experiences. Unsuccessful people view learning as a burden which stunts their growth and limits their influence. Throughout my experiences, I was sometimes successful and sometimes unsuccessful in relation to my desire to learn. I'm glad that I realized that I'd know enough when I know how to learn. But more importantly, I'm glad I know what I don't know, and that's what keeps the drive within me to learn tomorrow.

Question 4: Do you want to grow plants or people?

I heard an adage about growing people that has stuck with me: "If you want one year of success, grow grain. If you want ten years of success, grow trees. But if you want one hundred years of prosperity, grow people." That adage stuck with me because I'm all about growing people. I've learned to be an asset to those around me. People need to know they have value. I try to treat people the way I want them to be, not just the way they are. I believe people sometimes don't understand their value until someone else tells them their worth. When I was in elementary school, I can vividly remember shaking hands with our janitor. When he shook hands with the young boys, he would squeeze really hard. That didn't make sense to me until one day I asked him why he squeezed our hands so hard. The janitor said, "As a young man, always shake hands with a firm grip, and look people in the eyes when you do it. I want you young men to have confidence in yourselves." I didn't understand that then, but I understand it now. He was teaching us to have confidence in ourselves. Who would've ever thought that a mere handshake could teach confidence? He knew that eye contact was good for both self-respect and mutual respect.

It demonstrates that you are confident enough to look the other person in the eyes and that you are giving your full attention. In other words, he was more concerned with growing people even though we didn't know it at the time. He saw us as assets, and we were under his protection.

Success is always by design and not by chance. You can look at the life of any successful person in the world and almost always find a grateful attitude towards life. I would encourage you to reevaluate your beliefs and convictions and make sure they belong to you. I don't think anything will do more to derail your attempts at success than to have your beliefs and convictions conflict with reality or to have doubts about your own beliefs. If you can't verify your beliefs and convictions to your complete satisfaction, get rid of them and try something different based on your prior successes. Also, think about those four questions I considered to design success for my life. Are you a product of your environment? How important is your past to you? Do you want to learn tomorrow? And do you want to grow plants or people? You may not be able to answer those questions now, but I hope that you eventually can. However, you answer those questions, the results will be your success by design and not by chance.

Complete the Chapter Review below. Record and date your responses in a journal or composition notebook.

CHAPTER REVIEW

1. Does your personal/professional environment match or contradict the expectations of your behavior? If so, what can you do to make a difference in your environment?

2. What leadership lessons can you take from your past for success in your personal/professional life?

3. What can you to grow more people on a personal, professional, or spiritual path?

CHAPTER 5

CHANGE IS SCARY, BUT IT'S GOOD!

If you don't like something change it; if you can't change it, change the way you think about it.
—Mary Engelbreit

I can remember when I was young..." Those are the words I often hear adults use when comparing generations. I can remember reading a quote about being young that really made me laugh. Australian writer Germaine Greer said, "You are only young once, but you can be immature forever." I think there is something appealing in never having to grow up, as any fan of Bugs Bunny and Elmer Fudd can attest. But even though being young can be attractive, growing old and being immature is definitely not attractive at all. Eventually, I had to realize that change is scary, but it's good.

I can remember when I was growing up in the Mississippi Delta how I hated bees, but I later learned how much wisdom bees have. I hated bees because I only looked at them from a negative standpoint. I was never really fond of honey, and I was allergic to bee stings, but I eventually learned to like honey as I got older. I can remember when I stepped on a bee barefooted when I was 14. My foot had swollen up so big that I was not able to wear a shoe for a week. Needless to say, I was very young and immature in my thinking when I hated bees. But as I've gotten older, I've changed my thinking about bees because they are a perfect example as to how small things can make a big difference. I didn't realize that bees do all the things our parents did for us: provide shelter, care for their young, and provide other important necessities for life. Also as a natural instinct, bees work very hard to pollinate commercial crops. As author Michael O'Malley states in his book The Wisdom of Bees, one pound of honey requires fifty-five thousand miles of flight (one gallon requires one million miles) and the visitation of two million flowers. One teaspoon of honey represents the lifetime work of roughly a dozen bees. Worker honeybees live, on average, twenty-eight to thirty-five days, and six weeks longer in winter. Once I learned some facts about bees, I had to change my perspective about them and embrace it.

Bees are now one of my favorite insects to talk about regarding leadership and hard work.

Once I knew I couldn't change bees, I knew I had to change the way I thought about them. I learned that it took me reading about bees to change my thinking. I hope my experiences can help you change the way you think about those things that you can't change. As I discussed in the previous chapter, you can design success, but before mapping out my design, I had to change the way I viewed success to achieve success. Yes, change is scary, but it's good. I have written openly and honestly about how I used to be and why change was scary for me. I hope you can gain some valuable lessons from my experiences.

Growing up in the Delta, I thought everybody dressed like me, talked like me, liked everything I liked and was just like me in every other way. But as I got older and experienced more and more activities, it dawned on me that everything I knew in the Delta was just a snapshot of what life was really like everywhere else. I realized little by little with each life experience that I needed to change what I believed about myself and how I viewed the world, but it was very scary for me to do. There were five reasons why I didn't want to change when I was young: pride, laziness, rebellion, ignorance, and fear.

Pride: "I don't need to change."

I can remember playing in a basketball game in high school against one of our biggest rivals. We had practiced all week, and all week our coach told us to stay out of the corners when the other team pressed us. Of course, since I was the star player on the team, I thought that I was good enough to handle the press all by myself. So, we got in the game, and I handled the press all by myself for three-quarters. At the start of the fourth quarter, we were up five points, and I had all the confidence in the world to keep doing what I had done the first three-quarters. I thought to myself, "I don't need to change. I can keep doing what I'm doing." Well, the game ended with us losing by five points, and I had five turnovers. Those five turnovers I had came in the fourth quarter, and they also occurred in those corners our coach had told us to stay out of. What happened? Pride is what happened. It actually took me turning the ball over and losing the game before I would realize that I had too much pride to follow those simple instructions from our coach. I'm glad that I don't have too much pride now to change. I'm easily reminded of the downside of pride by the writings of King David in Proverbs 16:18 when he said, "Pride precedes a disaster, and an arrogant attitude precedes a fall." So, whenever I feel the need not to change because of pride, I think of those words.

Laziness: "It's hard to change."

I can tell now that I was being lazy about not wanting to follow the instructions of my coach. It was easy for me to do things my way. I didn't realize that he gave those directions for a specific reason. He knew the consequences of dribbling the ball to the corners and how it would eventually lead to turnovers, which would lead to the other team scoring, which would lead to us losing the game. At that time, I was lazy in my thinking and with my actions. My grandmother always reminded me what the Bible says about laziness in Proverbs 10:4: "Lazy hands make a man poor but diligent hands bring wealth." My grandmother always had a way of simplifying the most common concepts in the Bible. In Medea's words about laziness she said, "Don't ever let the sun bake your butt. When the sun rises, you need to rise." It didn't make sense then, but it makes sense now. She wanted to teach me not to be lazy. She wanted to teach me to get up and work for whatever I needed and wanted. I'm very thankful for those teachings. I just wish I would have transferred that knowledge and passion to that basketball game we lost.

Rebellion: "I don't want to change."

Have you ever heard the phrase, "A big fish is caught with big bait?" I had never heard that until the day I went fishing with a former boss of mine, Mr. Dan Jones. He passed away several years ago, and he was very instrumental in my life. We would always spend time fishing, and he would teach me a few things about fishing and life. On this particular day, we went bass fishing. Of course, I fished with my usual six-inch culprit worms because that's what I normally used. Mr. Dan, as I always called him, encouraged me to use some bigger worms to catch the bigger fish. I said, "Nawww, I'll use what I always use because I always catch big fish with the six-inch worms I use." He immediately said, "OK." So he fished with his fifteen-inch Berkley power baits, and I fished with my six-inch culprit worms. We both agreed we had a great day fishing as we counted twenty-six fish in the boat. I ended the day with fifteen bass with an average weight of three pounds. Mr. Dan ended the day with eleven bass with an average weight of seven pounds. I might have caught four more fish than he did but all of his fish were bigger than mine. How did he do that? I think there were two reasons my fish were not as big as Mr. Dan's fish. First, I was very rebellious in trying to do it the way I knew I had been successful with in the past. I did not want to try anything new because I was afraid of failure. Second, every time I saw him reel in a fish and I knew his catch was bigger than mine just at a glance. I was still rebellious in not changing my bait. This situation reminds me of how King Saul disobeyed God, and his rebellion cost him his kingship, his anointing, and his destiny. With that lesson learned today, I'm glad that I only lost some big fish versus losing my anointing and my destiny. I've learned not to be rebellious when people are sharing their knowledge and experience. I can honestly say that big fish are caught with big bait!

Ignorance: "I've never thought about changing."

Have you ever thought about the person you are? I have. After thoroughly considering, I was a lot like the comic strip character Charlie Brown. Charlie Brown is a lovable loser, a child possessed of endless determination and hope, but who is ultimately dominated by his insecurities.

One day after striking out in a baseball game, he says, "Rats! I'll never be a big-league player. I just don't have it! All my life I've dreamed of playing in the big leagues, but I'll never make it." His nemesis, Lucy, replies, "Charlie Brown, you're thinking too far ahead. What you need to do is set more immediate goals for yourself." For a moment, Charlie Brown sees a ray of hope by saying, "Immediate goals?" Lucy answers, "Yes, start with the next inning. When you go out to pitch, see if you can walk out to the mound without falling!"

Like I said earlier, I was once like Charlie Brown to an extent, but I learned that having people in my life like Lucy will not help me at all. Sometimes as individuals, insecurities can dominate and prevent change. I think it's important not to listen to the things people say if those things aren't encouraging. If the things they say are true but discouraging, examine if those people are actually trying to be constructive. I can normally sense when people care about me. How? When people tell me what they think the truth is, I sense with my heart. I always try to accept the truth but I can tell how and what people feel about me as they tell me the truth. Encouragement and the truth are what actually helped me consider changing who I was or who I wanted to be. I've been ignorant to the point of thinking that not knowing something was an excuse for not changing. Well, ignorance is not an excuse, and I'm glad that now I think every day about changing so I can be a better person. Your mind may fool you sometimes, but your heart never will. And it takes a very humble person to hear what others think the truth may be about you. So, think about the people in your life, and examine whether you need to make some changes. If you don't, maybe others will keep you confined by your insecurities the way Charlie Brown was confined by Lucy.

Fear: "I'm afraid to change."

I heard an old saying about fear that has stuck with me: "FEAR stands for False Expectations Appearing Real!" I believe people are afraid to change because the way they are appears to be real. At least that was my experience before I began to change as a person. I've learned that when you are afraid, you won't give your best. When you are afraid, fear will keep you from taking risks. When you are afraid to change, it will keep you in a box. I think being afraid to change will make your own closed perspective seem the right way to do things. Whenever I was afraid, I had believed that I was committed, devoted, and engaged in the activities I was involved in. Even though I made surface sacrifices, I was not making the right steps toward change. Sometimes when you are challenged by your loved ones to change, it causes you take a defensive stance and even come to believe that other people are against you.

So, I had to realize I had a problem of not changing. The book Leadership and Self-Deception says about getting out of the box, "Identify someone with a problem and you'll be identifying someone who resists the suggestion that he has a problem. That's self-deception—the inability to see that one has a problem." I'm glad that I decided to get out of the box and get over the fear of changing who I was. I like the old saying, "No one tests the depth of a river with both feet." So just know that all change does not lead to improvement, but all improvements are caused by change. I'm realizing more and more that change is not an event; it's a process that sometimes takes your entire life. I'm glad that I'm constantly looking fear in the eyes and facing it head on.

I had to start confronting the brutal truths of who I was before I could start the process of changing as a person. When it came to pride, I knew I had it, but I had to change the way I thought about it. You know, no one ever choked to death by swallowing his pride. When it came to laziness, I knew I was lazy, so I had to learn to work hard. You know it's easy to be lazy when you don't know or accept the truth. When it came to rebellion, I eventually realized that my loved ones want to help me and not harm me. I have firsthand experience that big fish are caught with big bait. When it came to ignorance, I had to learn what I didn't know. Admitting that you don't know something is important. Rejecting something you know nothing about is the greatest ignorance. When it came to fear, I had to realize how it stunted my growth. Fear for me has been a very large shadow that is very small in might! It has taken honest and diligent effort for me to determine the truth of who I am. I hope my experiences can help you realize that if you don't like who you are, change the way you think about yourself because although change can be very scary, it can also be very good!

Complete the Chapter Review below. Record and date your responses in a journal or composition notebook.

CHAPTER REVIEW

1. What is your biggest fear about changing the person you have become?

2. Name 3-5 things that you don't know how to do that you would like to be able to do.

3. Name three things you know you need to change within the next 1-3 years.

CHAPTER 6

OK! MEANS OPPORTUNITY KNOCKING

Learn everything you can, anytime you can, from anyone you can—there will always come a time when you will be grateful you did.

—*Sarah Caldwell*

There's a story about a lumberjack who was supposed to be the best in the land because he had won many competitions. This lumberjack used an axe that was sharpened to perfection. He used the methods that were passed down from previous generations. Of course, he was in the prime of his life and very strong, but he never changed his techniques or invested in new or updated technology. One day a very thin young man challenged him to a tree falling contest. The lumberjack laughed and took the bet. As they both faced their respective trees, the starter yelled, "On your marks, get set, go!" The young man smiled as he drop-started his chainsaw with enthusiasm. The lumberjack dropped his axe and with a strange look on his face yelled, "What is that noise?!"

Are there people around you who are like that lumberjack—are personally limited by their resistance to change and confined to their comfort zone? Those limited people don't appreciate the benefits of lifelong learning. According to Marc Revere, fire chief of the Novato Fire Protection District in Marin County, California, people fail to understand the concept of "accept, adapt and accelerate—or die." Like the lumberjack, they fail to even realize that reality has already set in.

So like I shared in the previous chapter, change is scary, but it can also be good. By now you can see, my upbringing was somewhat similar to the lumberjack's, and it might not have been that different from yours. But I knew I had to look at which direction to take next to recognize the opportunities knocking before me. I always had opportunities before me, but at times they seemed to get fuzzy as I tried to keep track of where I have been and try to prepare for what was coming next. Even though I did things differently from others in my family such as being the first to fly on a plane and the first to leave the county, I constantly had to fight off the tendency to follow a similar mindset of the previous generations like the lumberjack. Now back to the lumberjack's question, "What's that noise?" From my perspective that noise has always come from two components: discipline and discernment.

Of course, I was forced to learn discipline as a young man growing up in the dusty flatlands of the Mississippi Delta. My grandmother taught me to work at a young age, the importance of being on time, to finish what I started, to be dependable, and to be organized. She had to have the discipline to teach me those things. And of course, I didn't have a choice in learning it. I learned at an early age that discipline was all about getting certain behaviors and attitudes to translate into successful routines in life. In other words, if I didn't do things a certain way, my grandmother would have some consequences for my lack of actions or lack of enthusiasm in my actions. I learned at an early age that there were no shortcuts to any place worth going.

According to author Paul Meyer, in his book Unlocking Your Legacy: 25 Keys for Success, discipline is created, it isn't somewhere waiting to be discovered. My grandmother taught me that discipline was not about punishment, but it was about self-control. It was about disciplined thinking leading to disciplined actions. She didn't call it discipline at the time; she just was firm and stern in her directions. I truly believe that any success I've had has been a result of being disciplined in my thinking first. I've always had to ask myself, "Who am I and what is my purpose?" Of course, the answers have changed over the years, but I do understand the process now. I believe my purpose was found at the crossroads of the things I've been passionate about and the things that I am somewhat good at. I was passionate about athletics, and I am somewhat successful at getting a good education. Once my purpose and the kind of person I wanted to become was apparent, I had to discipline my thinking to be a selfless person rather than focusing on achieving trappings like money, fame, and other things that will eventually fade away. I'm proud to be a lifelong learner by volunteering and serving in my community. I believe that over time, my thoughts and behaviors nourished and expanded my God-given purpose for a greater calling.

Of course, it helps when you have someone like my grandmother in your life to help you with the discipline process. Madea's guidance helped me to understand what discipline is all about. I like to read about others that have experienced situations like mine. For example, Kurt Kaiser, one of the leading composers of Christian music, is a great example of how discipline can lead to a successful life. He practiced five hours at the piano every day beginning when he was three years old. He learned as a child to believe in himself and believe in the things he was doing. His dad helped in the process, as Kaiser admits, "My dad would threaten to tie my leg to the piano stool if I didn't play five hours. I cannot remember a day when I did not play five hours." He attributes his success today to the discipline he learned as a child. I can relate to stories like Kurt Kaiser's. When I was ten years old, I learned to wash my own clothes and cook a basic meal for myself. My grandmother was very instrumental in that process. I had to have all of my clothes washed, dried, and folded before I could go out to play on the weekend. The washing process was very long, and I had to dry my clothes outside on a clothesline because we didn't have a dryer. And sometimes, it took the entire weekend to complete that whole task. When it came to cooking, I learned how to cook breakfast, lunch, and dinner. I believe that's why I love to cook now as an adult. During that time growing up with my grandmother, I thought I was learning how to take care of myself and not be dependent on any other person. Today, I realize that my grandmother was not only teaching me how to care for myself, but she was also teaching me how to be a helpmate for my future wife. I know my wife, Sarah, appreciates the discipline my grandmother taught me.

Now back to the lumberjack's original question again, "What's that noise?" From my perspective, the other component of that noise has always been the ability to discern. My grandmother was very wise when it came to discerning certain things about people. She would tell me, "Birds of a feather flock together." That's a very common saying, but it makes a lot of sense. She wanted me to be very cautious about the people I spent a lot of time with. She always taught me that it was not about judging people but about taking care of myself. She would say that people would tell me anything to convince me to do what they wanted me to do. She wanted me to know how to trust people who would have respect for my best interest and not trust those who had a focus on a selfish interest. I learned that my trust had to be earned just like I had to earn the trust of others.

She also taught me how to take advantage of opportunities by trying to see the good in any situation. When the basketball coaches from the University of Southern Mississippi came to our home to offer me a scholarship, she was very wise in her observations. When the coaches expressed their interest in signing me to a scholarship, my grandmother had some very discerning words for me that I'll never forget. It didn't matter that those coaches were in the room, and it didn't matter that they had just made me feel like I was the best player they would ever sign to a scholarship. Madea looked me in the eyes and said, "Sam, even though you are a very good basketball player, you are a horrible defensive player." Of course, all the coaches laughed when she said that, but it was humbling for me. My grandmother's discerning spirit put me on notice that I still had improvements to make even though I was receiving praise from the coaches. Madea recognized that the coaches knew I was a good player, but she wanted me to recognize that a good player doesn't equal a great player. She reminded me that even though I was being offered this scholarship, I still needed to work on other things on the court. Madea had my best interest in mind and, needless to say, I understood that I need to have a discerning mind and to take advantage of the opportunities placed before me.

I'm also inspired by the memorable events in the lives of others. In my opinion, without hesitation, the FedEx Corporation has been one of my favorite success stories of the past quarter-century because one man had a discerning spirit about opportunities. Fred W. Smith created an overnight delivery service when he recognized the demands in the shipping service arena. He wrote a term paper for an economics class during his undergraduate studies at Yale in 1965. Smith argues that he probably made a C on the paper, but he insists that he made a very simple observation:

As society became more automated, companies like IBM and Xerox that sold early computer devices needed to make sure their products were dependable. As companies began to put computers in banks to cancel checks—rather than clerks—or people began to put sophisticated electronics in airplanes—society and the manufacturers of that automated society were going to need a completely different logistics system. They had to be 100% reliable, or the efficacy of the device was in question.

I first read the FedEx story after I finished college. This story inspired me because when I was in college, I was just glad to get a C on any of my work. The FedEx story is just a great example of how you need to realize that every situation that occurs is just another opportunity knocking and presenting a possibility for success. I didn't realize all the opportunities I had knocking when I was in college. Some of those opportunities included participating in student organizations and other campus community service projects. But I do understand those opportunities now that I've graduated.

As you respond to your own opportunities knocking, keep in mind that you have to grasp the concept of knowing what changes you need to make to take advantage of these sometimes loud and sometimes quiet opportunities. Opportunities knocking are those chances we get to succeed. Opportunities are normally dressed up as a chance at hard work. I believe it's important to understand that whatever you put your hands to, work hard and give it all that you have. As Apostle Elder Richard G. Scott once stated, "In quiet moments when you think about it, you recognize what is critically important in life and what isn't. Be wise and don't let good things crowd out those that are essential." As I've searched for my own opportunities knocking, good things sometimes clouded my judgment and caused me to think I was doing what I needed to be doing. My basketball career is a perfect example of that. I was fortunate enough to begin to not only listen to what God wanted me to do through that phase of my life but eventually act on what He wanted me to do. And even with that, I had to have discipline and discernment through those times. I've learned a lot, and I know there's much more for me to learn. If you look at anyone who has reached the highest level of a profession, discipline has always played a major role in reaching that point. Without discipline, success usually will not last, and that is the biggest difference between being good and being great. Author H. Jackson Brown insists that "talent without discipline is like an octopus on roller skates. There's plenty of movement, but you never know if it's going to be forward, backward, or sideways." You have to be able to discern things about situations to realize the opportunities before you. Most people make the mistake of planning only by what they know. I've learned the trick is to lay out what you know against all there is to know, take out the overlap, and then try to find out as much as possible of what you still need to know. In reality, that is what discernment is all about. That's why and how FedEx came into existence.

There is a popular story describing a frog slowly being boiled alive. The premise is that if a frog is placed in boiling water, it will jump out, but if it is placed in cold water that is slowly heated, it will not perceive the danger and will be cooked to death. The story is often used as a metaphor for the inability of people to react to significant changes that occur gradually and to realize the opportunities before them. So as you continue to search throughout your life for opportunities you are faced with in life—good, bad or indifferent—realize that some people may say it's just noise, but realize that it could be another chance for greatness in your life.

Complete the Chapter Review below. Record and date your responses in a journal or composition notebook.

CHAPTER REVIEW

1. Identify 3 opportunities that have been before you that you have not taken advantage of.

2. What do you need (physical, financial, people resources) in order to take advantage of these opportunities?

3. What are you next steps in moving forward to take action in making the opportunities give you your desired results?

CHAPTER 7

THE MAKING OF A CHAMPION: FROM INSPIRATION TO APPLICATION

Champions know that success is inevitable; that there is no such thing as failure, only feedback. They know that the best way to forecast the future is to create it.

—*Michael J. Gelb*

I was born in the small Mississippi Delta town of Shelby on April 24, 1974. That was a very significant year, not only because I was born but because of the historic boxing match between Muhammad Ali and George Foreman hyped as the Rumble in the Jungle. How is a boxing match related the story of my life? Well, I view it as an important example of how champions are made, and that particular fight can be a lesson about how to win in life. This particular fight is a story of how a victory, whether great or small, can excite others, and it still encourages me today. I believe Muhammad Ali is the greatest fighter that ever lived. He had a very charismatic attitude that made people either like him or hate him. I also believe the Rumble in the Jungle was one of his most magical performances because he showed humility and determination to win. The fight was in the city of Kinshasa, Zaire, the heart of the jungle. Ali faced the reigning world heavyweight champion, George Foreman. Foreman was considered one of the hardest hitters during that time and Ali was considered a major underdog.

Leading up to the fight, Ali declared he was going to dance and use his speed to keep away from Foreman and outbox him, but his strategy changed during the bout. Ali began the fight going after Foreman and landing some punches which caught Foreman off guard. Foreman then began to use his experience in an attempt to knock Ali out. Foreman had won 37 of his 40 bouts by knockout, mostly within three rounds, and eight of his previous bouts didn't go past the second round. Ali was hoping for an opportunity to outlast Foreman.

As Foreman punched his way through earlier rounds, Ali resisted by ducking the worst of his punches and leaning against the ropes protecting his face with his elbows, a technique that later came to be known as "rope-a-dope." And as the rope-a-dope was in effect, Ali began a verbal assault with sarcastic remarks like, "Is that all you got, George? I thought you were supposed to be bad." Even though Ali paid the price by taking Foreman's body shots, Ali knew he was wearing Foreman down. No one knew at the time what Ali was doing, not even his trainer Angelo Dundee. I don't believe his fans knew what Ali had planned, but he continued to work and wait for his opportunity.

As Foreman continued to tire, his face became damaged by the hard and fast jabs that Ali threw. As the fight progressed, it was evident that Ali's tactics were taking their toll on Foreman. Ali allowed Foreman to wear himself out because Ali was only taking Foreman's best punches. And when Foreman tired out, Ali figured that's when he would make his move.

Before he would make his move, Ali continued more with verbal assaults such as, "They told me you could punch, George! They told me you could punch as hard as Joe Louis." Next, Ali hit Foreman with several right hooks and a few combinations that caused Foreman to stumble to the canvas. The fight was over. This fight has since become one of the most distinguished fights in history because it resulted in Ali, against the odds, regaining the title against a younger and stronger Foreman.

Of course at the time of this fight, I was five months old but every time I read the transcript or see video clips I get excited. As I've gone through life, I've been fortunate enough to study the lives and times of people like Muhammad Ali and every time I am encouraged by the events of their lives because I can relate. In this particular fight, Ali showed how you could go about and take punishment knowing that you will make a great comeback. It showed that even when your opponent has the upper hand, there is always time to redeem yourself. Ali did just that. He can be an example to each of us—willing to be seen as nothing, taking his opponents best shot, to become the greatest. Ali said it then, "I am the greatest; I said that even before I knew I was." Ali didn't surrender that evening but every time I watch that fight, it's as if I don't know the outcome, and I expect him to surrender. Every time I see that great comeback, it's like he's letting a winning horse out of its stall at the Kentucky Derby, and it fills me with admiration. I am still today encouraged by this particular fight and how he has continued to live his life with such grace. As you can see, a victory like the Rumble in the Jungle can have a long-lasting effect.

I think that's what each of us should do. We should never be afraid to be seen as nothing to become something greater than we ever imagined we could be. Remembering that if we follow our convictions through each challenging event and every obstacle before us can impact the lives of others. The Rumble in the Jungle still has an impact on my life today because of the humility Ali showed. He

The Man I Never Knew

Samuel L. Jones, Ph.D.

showed humility by allowing himself to take the best of his opponent. Ali knew what Foreman's strengths and weaknesses were. I believe that is how he was able to show humility. If you don't show humility, then it's hard for you to understand your opponent's strengths and weaknesses. Ali used Foreman's strengths and weaknesses against him. One thing I learned from this fight is you must always accept your opponents' best because that is the only way to win. Once you get to know your opponents' best, then you know how you can apply their weakness against their strengths.

When I was growing up in the Delta, I had dreams of being inspiring like Muhammad Ali which lead me to try to apply certain characteristics to my life such as humility and hard work. But I didn't realize that even in Ali's trash talking throughout his career, he still displayed some sense of humility. I believe the sooner young people find humility, the easier it will become for them to be successful. As adults, we want to force humility on them, but I know that experience is the best teacher. Some people may think they have a degree of humility, but they won't until the roller coaster ride of life starts giving them the unexpected. I'm fortunate enough to have experienced a few things that have taught me humility.

When I first got to the University of Southern Mississippi in the fall of 1992 as a freshman, I had two such challenging experiences. The first was related to my roommate, George Scott, who was competing for the same starting position on the basketball team. This was when I first learned to leave my competition on the court, to have a friendship off the court, and to have some humility. For me, the first day our team played an unofficial scrimmage game was very humbling. When I was in high school, I was the best player or, as some would say, the stud. I did it all. I scored. I stole the ball. I blocked shots. I was named the MVP because I did it all. But in 1992, I was a freshman playing with other freshmen, sophomores, juniors, and seniors in college. It didn't take me long to realize that I wasn't the best player on the court anymore. It didn't take long for me to realize that I was just an average player. After the first few days of scrimmaging, I was demoralized because I realized I had to make a very tough decision. Do I leave school because I'm not good enough or do I stay and fight for playing time to get better on the court? That's a question I had to answer for myself. I believe most college freshmen athletes eventually have to make tough decisions at some point in their college career. I believe this is because the pressures and demands of college athletics are entirely different from those in high school. In college, most everyone that you compete against is bigger, faster, and stronger and, more importantly, more experienced than you are. And every time you compete, you have to play hard and fast because everyone else was also the best the player on the high school team.

My issues on the court also affected me in the classroom. All of my classes were going well with the exception of my speech class. I was affected the most in this class because of my lack of self-confidence and because of the challenges of being in a new environment. My high school graduating class had about 150 graduates. USM had about thirteen thousand students my freshman year. In high school, I knew all of my classmates, the teachers, and the administrators. But when I got to college, the only people I knew were my basketball teammates and most of the football team. I only knew the football team because we lived in the same dorm. I eventually reached out to other students as my college experience evolved but I didn't get involved in student life in college as I should have. I believe student life activities like Student Government Association and other groups on campus could have helped me feel less stressed, but I thought I didn't have time for those organizations.

The stress of academics and athletics eventually took its toll on me. I hated that speech class because it forced me to speak in front a room full of people I didn't know even though I had a stuttering problem. Every Tuesday and Thursday, when I had that class, I felt as if I would have a heart attack. The nervousness and anxiety I had from that class and my pending decision about basketball were unbearable. My frustrations with how basketball practice was going and the demands of my speech class presented me with a fork in the road. I describe any situation as a "fork in the road" when I get to a point where life-changing decisions will have to be made. I had to make these decisions on my own, and I have never told anyone about these frustrations until now. My choice regarding basketball was to quit the team and go back to the Delta to do something else or to stay at USM and fight for playing time. When I look back, I can't believe I even contemplated dropping out of college and leaving a scholarship behind because I was dealt some tough blows as an eighteen-year-old. As for my speech class, I had to decide if I would keep the class to maintain twelve credit hours. If I dropped below the twelve-hour threshold, I would be giving up my eligibility for the basketball team. Needless to say, the decisions to stay on the basketball team and stay in the speech class were connected. One decision would eventually affect the other. I decided to stay on the team and compete for playing time against my roommate. George and I remained on the team, and we remained roommates. I went on to start twenty games out of the twenty-seven-game season, and I made the conference all-tournament freshmen team. Today, my former roommate, George, is one of my best friends. As for that speech class, I ended the semester with a D and long with low self-esteem because of my beliefs about my stuttering problem.

The Man I Never Knew	Samuel L. Jones, Ph.D.

You see, sometimes we believe that our problems define us. I had to learn that my problem didn't define me, it made me discover what was in me. I later retook the class and got an A. I'm glad I retook that class because it allowed me to discover my confidence in my abilities as a public speaker.

I've learned through my personal experiences with my athletic and my academic career that I'm fortunate enough to have this platform where I can share my thoughts to inspire others. Some may see my experience with basketball or my experience with a speech class as a small victory, but I see it as an example for others to focus on the process of working hard, especially with the opportunities that are before them. It took me some time to realize that it's great to be inspired and encouraged by things in life, but at some point, you have to get down to the nitty-gritty of getting things done and have some humility along the way. I've learned that inspiration without application is just a happy, exciting hallucination which can eventually encourage you to give up in life. I've seen people that are so inspired that they forget they have to go to work the next day. Then I've seen people that don't care about being inspired, they just work and don't live the experience of working with people and realizing those people need inspiration. I believe inspiration (encouragement) and application (hard work) must go hand and hand for you to become your best. I've also learned that only when you are humble can you objectively examine what happened to you and why. You might come to find that you're not perfect, and you have plenty of room for improvement. The biggest room we all have is room for improvement. I truly hope my experiences will help others examine their own personal experiences to be motivated, to be inspired, and to be humble and work hard. So whenever I'm inspired by a song, a movie, or a good book, I try to grasp the points that will help me apply sound objectives to my life. If I don't, I'll find myself misleading myself which leads to a place I'd rather not be.

The making of a champion has to start somewhere. I've learned that it takes things happening in your life that get your attention before you can recognize what exactly to do next. I truly believe you have to be inspired before you can apply yourself to do anything. And sometimes that inspiration may come at the most unexpected time. According to "The Muhammad Ali Biography" on the Biography Channel website, Muhammad Ali discovered his talent for boxing through an odd twist of fate when he was twelve. His bike was stolen, and Ali told a police officer, Joe Martin, that he wanted to beat up the thief. Martin said, "Well, you better learn how to fight before you start challenging people." In addition to being a police officer, Martin also trained young boxers at a local gym. So it took Ali's bike being stolen for him to realize his talent for fighting. For me, I had to get to the point of being frustrated with a speech class and competing on the basketball court before I would find my desire for public speaking and sharing my personal experiences to inspire others to be their best. But it also took some humility. So whatever it takes to inspire you, be sure you challenge and apply yourself and have plenty of humility along the way. I've learned that some people change because they see the light, and others change because they feel the heat, and some don't change at all. So the next time you are frustrated with your personal goals, remember the words of boxing great Muhammad Ali, "I hated every minute of training, but I said, 'Don't quit. Suffer now and live the rest of your life as a champion.'" Keep in mind that a victory, whether great or small, can excite others. So whatever your training is (school, work, your role as father, mother, brother, sister, etc.) suffer now and live the rest of your life as a champion because that is the true making of a champion, from inspiration to application.

Complete the Chapter Review below. Record and date your responses in a journal or composition notebook.

CHAPTER REVIEW

1. Identify three events in your life that have inspired you to activate your desire to take a chance on a new opportunity.

CHAPTER 8

YOUR TIPPING POINT IS YOUR NEXT STEP

There are things which must cause you to lose your reason or you have none to lose. An abnormal reaction to abnormal situation is normal behavior.

—*Viktor E. Frankl*

When I first thought about writing this book, I wanted to share my personal experiences to encourage others who may have dealt with experiences similar to mine. I've struggled with the question, "Do I share ALL my personal experiences or do I share only the ones that affected me the most?" I decided I would only share the ones that affected me the most, but as I've gone through the process of writing each chapter, I've learned to pour my soul into each one because that's what God told me to do. I could hear gentle reminders of my grandmother telling me what the Bible says in Matthew 5:14-16: "A city on a hill cannot be hidden. No one lights a lamp and puts it under a bowl; instead, it is put on the lamp stand, where it gives light for everyone in the house. In the same way your light must shine before people, so that they will see the good things you do and praise your Father in heaven." I believe we all have a light so we need to use it and let it shine so others can see our works and where our strength comes from even when we've struggled through life. But if there is any praise to be given, don't praise me, praise my Father in heaven because he has given me the strength to endure life's struggles, both big and small.

You may wonder what that has to do with how your tipping point is your next step. Well, first, I'll explain the concept of a tipping point and why it's important in life. Then, I'll share one major experience and how it has affected me. And last, I'll talk about vision and making people matter. I hope your curiosity will be filled from there.

In 2000, Malcolm Gladwell's book The Tipping Point offered readers a ground-breaking analysis of how trends are sparked and then take hold in society. The book became a national bestseller which influenced paradigm shifts in American culture. The nature of modern culture is such that many new ideas are constantly introduced from a variety of sources. Some of these ideas achieve success through popularity and influence while others fail because of popularity and influence. Even though the tipping point is a concept for society, you can apply it to your personal life.

Gladwell identifies three key factors which play a role in determining whether a particular trend will "tip" into wide-scale influence and popularity: the concepts of the Law of the Few, the Stickiness Factor, and the Power of Context. The Law of the Few contends that a few key people must champion an idea, concept or product before it can reach the tipping point. If the idea, concept or product is endorsed, it is more likely that it will tip into success. The Stickiness Factor is the quality that compels people to pay close, sustained attention to an idea, concept or product. Stickiness is normally unconventional, unexpected and contrary to perceived wisdom. The Power of Context insists that the environment, conditions, and circumstances are vital in determining if an idea, concept, or product will tip. The Power of Context is probably the most important factor of the three.

So why are these points important in your personal life? They are important because you need to understand how we all are influenced by culture. That's why it's also important to know that as humans, we need a higher power to be influenced by and that is God. As for my life,

I've needed God more than anyone can ever imagine. Yes, I've experienced some success with my education and with my professional life, but my tipping point in my life has always been my next step. The only thing different now from twenty years ago is that I now understand that my spiritual life should be the foundation for everything I believe and act upon.

As you may have noticed, I haven't mentioned anything about my father throughout this book. You may have wondered why. Well, I have no idea who he is. Let me repeat that: I have no idea who my father is. By my admitting that at thirty-six years old, I've made great strides to not only acknowledge that, but to live with it. So my tipping point has always been learning how to deal with it, which was part of the next step. I learned that some of the steps I was taking led me to be influenced by things that didn't matter. It also led me to ignore the facts in hopes that they'd go away. The hardest part about not knowing who my father is has been the struggle to understand how I've become the man I am without him in my life. These thoughts didn't really become as important until I reached adulthood and began to have the desire to start my own family. Not having my father in my life while I was growing up had a huge impact on me. I never had a birthday party with my father. I never went fishing with my father. I never saw him smile when I scored my first points on the basketball court. I never got that encouragement of a hug or to hear him say the words, "Son, I'm proud of you." Even through the process of writing this book, I still wonder if he even knows that I exist. Those are things I've always wondered, but I never got answers to. My mom did her best to explain the circumstances, but there are things in life that sometimes only time can fix. I'm thankful that, even in this situation, my mom and I are still able to have a loving relationship. The only thing I know about him is his name and that he went to Jackson State University with my mom in the early 1970s. I don't know if he knows about me, but I hope this book is a way to notify him that I'm reaching out to him. Even with that said I had to realize that this void created by my father's absence would never go away until I accepted it and moved on with my life. So as I've embraced my father's absence, my hope is that once this book is published, a gateway to a relationship with him would have opened for me because this book made it possible. I believe this book could make it possible because it has allowed me to share my suffering and my desire to help someone else that may have experienced something similar. And who knows, maybe my father will read this book one day and be encouraged to reach out to me. And maybe my readers could be encouraged to experience a better relationship with God based on their experiences. My desire is to use my adversity to help others deal with their own.

To help me accept my father's absence and begin the process of moving forward, I applied Gladwell's concepts. Gladwell's factor the Law of the Few says that a few key people must champion an idea, concept or product before it can reach the tipping point. For me, the Law of the Few means that if everyone is buying into a single idea or concept, then I need to rethink my acceptance of it. I was always the kind of person that never went with the crowd. If it takes me standing out in a crowd to be different because I differ from the crowd, then that is what I'll do. French philosopher Henri-Louis Bergson said, "A person should think like a man of action—act like a man of thought." I had to gain wisdom to understand that the crowd is what makes an idea tip, and that's how trends are started. So I had to decide who would be in my crowd. First, I had to think about who the few key people in my life were who could champion the idea that I must move past this misfortune in my life about not knowing who my father is. In no particular order, my crowd consisted of my wife, my mother, my former basketball coach, my parents-in-law, my pastor, and my grandmother.

My first key person was my wife, Sarah. She has always been supportive of me in everything I've ever done or wanted to do. I believe that beside every good man is a good woman. So men, if you think you're a good man, check to see if you have a good woman beside you supporting your efforts. Sarah has supported me in my professional arena, but it means much more from a personal standpoint. From the first moment I saw her, I knew she was a special person. She was so special that the first moment I saw her I said to myself in a calm, relaxed voice, "She's going to be my wife." This happened as she walked by while I was working in a retail store. Fortunately, she came back to the store, we exchanged phone numbers, and we were able to get to know each other. I still joke now that I believe the only reason she came back to the store is that she saw me, too and that she said, "He's going to be my husband." A year later, we were married. And we've been married sixteen years since. From our first moments of deep, thoughtful conversations, I told her of the absence of my father. She never judged me, my family or my situation, and I appreciate that. She always encouraged me and supported me in my efforts to locate my father. She has helped me deal with this tipping point in my life. And not only that, she continues to support anything that I do. Her compassion for me, a man with a void in his life, allowed me to fall deeply in love with her, and I want that love to remain and grow.

My next key person was my mother. I believe my mother has done the best she could for me throughout my life. I'm thankful to this day for her love and support. I hope that if you might have conflicts, misunderstandings, or disagreements with your parents, that you please get beyond those and learn to forgive and love them while you have them in your life. I believe that there are some relationships, even those between a parent and a child, that are so toxic that it is healthier to forgive, but to recognize that the relationship is not salvageable. I've always believed that my relationship with my mother is salvageable, so that's why I continue to focus on the present instead of the past when it comes to my relationship with her. I haven't always had that hope, but Madea would help me keep things in perspective. Whenever my grandmother would sense that I was upset with my mom, she would remind me of what the Bible says in Ephesians 6:2-3: "Honor your father and mother"—which is the first commandment with a promise—"so that it may go well with you and that you may enjoy long life on the earth." So no matter what happened in the past, I will always love, honor, and respect my mother.

My next key person was my high school basketball coach Willie Earl Thomas. I believe Coach Thomas was probably the first man in my life to help me learn how to handle adversity. As I mentioned in an earlier chapter, Coach Thomas saw some talent in me when I was a seventh-grader. I didn't think I was a good player, but he thought I was. He gave me a chance to prove myself by playing with the varsity team. I can remember how excited I was when I made the team. As the season progressed, I can remember one situation in particular which changed my outlook. We had lost a ball game on the road, and most of my teammates were talking about quitting the team. Of course, I joined in complaining and eventually thought about quitting the team.

Coach Thomas overheard, and he had a soft and somber conversation with me that changed my outlook, not just on basketball, but on life in general. He told me that I was a leader and that I shouldn't follow anyone who wanted to give up. He told me that "in life, things will always get tough, and that's how you find out what kind of person you are." As I look back on that experience now, I've learned that people quit when they want the easy way out. I've always remembered that Coach Thomas was the main reason I didn't quit the basketball team because he had faith in me as a person first, then as a basketball player. I can honestly say that even though my father wasn't there, Coach Thomas stood in his place on several occasions, and I will always be grateful for that.

My Mother, Girte Jones (left); My Wife, Sarah Jones (right); My doctoral graduation from Mississippi State University in 2006.

My next key people were my parents-in-law. I believe in giving praise and honor where they are due, and they deserve every bit of that giving and then some. MC and Dorothy Clark have been a perfect example of what marriage should be. They've been married for thirty-eight years, and they continue to be an example of what love is. Mrs. Clark has always encouraged me to press forward and to allow my faith to be the foundation for everything that I do. And Mr. Clark is another father figure who lives out daily what fatherhood is all about. The thing I like best about him is that he doesn't do a lot of talking. He lives out what he believes, and that is very refreshing, and I've learned so much from him. They have supported Sarah and me from the first day we were married. Even before we got married, they had already treated me like family which was encouraging. I've always believed that a relationship with in-laws is just like marriage, you can make it what you want it to be. I can honestly say that I married into a God-fearing family, and they treat me like a son. I try my best to treat them like parents. I hope others can experience that same joy with their families at some point in their lives.

Another key person in my life who supported me through this void was my pastor, Rev. Walter L. Moore. It's easy for me to say that the sermons he preached on Sundays helped me deal with my tipping point in my life by encouraging me, motivating me, and giving me hope. But it was also those conversations around the dinner table or just those conversations standing around after church services that had such a profound effect. I appreciate him as a man, a father figure, a true leader, and a true friend, and he has always made a positive influence on my life. I'm very thankful that he is my spiritual leader.

Another important person in my life was my grandmother, Madea. As you've may have noticed throughout this book, Madea showed up in every facet of my life. I'm just thankful that she poured her soul into raising me to be a humble, hard-working man who cares about people. If you still have your grandparents in your life, I would encourage you to spend as much time with them as possible. Get a recorder and sit at their feet and allow them to pour their wisdom into your life.

All the people in my crowd were in a position to help me to gain and keep perspective of who I am. They all had the ability to help me gain perspective by helping me to keep my faith and rely on it even when I might question it. And also, they helped me to continue to be humble with my experiences by encouraging me to remember where I came from. I don't think it was one particular thing they each did; I think it was a combination of all their efforts.

Each of these people had the ability to apply what Gladwell calls the Stickiness Factor for me. Each of them compelled me to pay close, sustained attention to the concept of trusting and having faith in God to provide all my needs. It has taken some time for me to realize that the absence of my father was a major tipping point in my life. As I've grown into adulthood, my life experiences and the people around me helped me realized that God has provided everything I need or could ever imagine needing even despite the absence of a father. One thing I can appreciate is that I have had several male role models in my life to help me understand how to be a strong, secure, God-fearing man who loves his family. I use to see myself as unimportant because of the lack of a relationship with my father. I use to get depressed or frustrated when I would see young men with strong relationships with their fathers. I had to learn to make my situation special and important to me, and I would advise other males not to take their relationships with their fathers for granted. I've learned that a man who knows that accepting himself as important and valuable is worth far more than just a man merely trying to improve himself in the eyes of others. I use to try to improve myself for other people—to fit in or to look good in a way others would notice. But I had to get to know myself at an intimate level that was not for external approval or the perceptions of others. To become a man, the apostle Paul indicated we must be willing to stop thinking as children and learn to accept who we are. Proverbs 23:7 says, "As a man thinks in his heart, so he is." I'm thankful that I have positive views of myself and that I can send that positive vibe to others. I now know that I'm important and valuable in my own special way because I know I will always have something to offer. So now when I see other males with their fathers, I feel proud because I see positive influences instead of thinking about my situation. Needless to say, I don't hold any negative feelings about my situation anymore. I believe God has placed the right people around me to support me through this journey, and this is why I want to help others through theirs.

Gladwell's last factor is the Power of Context which he says is probably the most important. I've had to put all of my personal experiences into context because my thoughts, ideas, and life experiences will always be very different from those of someone who has not experienced what I have. My situation has continued to keep me humble, so I know it's easy to say I don't understand how and why someone else made one choice over the other. My experience has helped me not judge anyone because I will never completely understand the context of their situation at any given time. But my experience has allowed me to be patient and still show kindness.

So how do you learn not to judge others? There are two ways I keep from judging others. First, I try to always consider my vision. I've learned that if I stay focused on my vision, then I don't have the insight to judge anyone else. I always ask myself is my vision is big enough. If my vision is big enough, then it should always include me helping others and others helping me. Whether it's giving or receiving help, there is never any time or desire to judge others. Matthew 7:1 tells us to judge not so that God will not judge you; for God will judge you in the same manner you judge others. I encourage you to think about that the next time you either ask someone for help, or you give someone help. Judgment rarely comes to my mind. Judgment normally comes to mind when you don't want to give help, or no one wants to help you. So always consider your vision and make sure other people are included in it. If your vision does not include either you helping others or others helping you, then your vision is not big enough.

The second way I've learned not to judge others is to always make people matter. I've learned that you make people matter by the way you serve them. When I was younger, my grandmother would ask me to do small things like get her a glass of water or split fire wood. She would watch my attitude in how I approached each task, how I did the task, and how I completed the task. Some days I was thrilled to do as she asked and other days I acted as if it would kill me to fill even the simplest requests. But as I got older and before she passed away, I learned to appreciate the opportunity to do anything for her because I learned that it was my way of serving her in some small capacity. Author Patrick Lencioni said when he graduated from college that he "wanted to change the world." He went on to say that he didn't think about two fundamental matters because they weren't important at the time: "Who are the people I'm serving? And am I ready to suffer?" I believe we are all here to serve in some capacity whether it has a title or not. I believe the highest among all titles is servant. But for you to serve in that capacity, you have to not only know the people you are serving, but you must also know their needs. You have to be very attentive to small details to know their needs. When I was with my grandmother, I didn't focus on her needs because I was thinking about my own. I believe she imparted so much wisdom that I am still learning to appreciate it all even now.

And, like Lencioni said, are you ready to suffer? I believe because of the advancements in technology and modern science, we have been lured into thinking that we don't need to suffer for anything. I believe that when you put people first, you don't think about your suffering. For example, one thing I always try to do is to test my patience for the sake of others. If I'm in the grocery store or wherever there is a line, I try to always allow others to go ahead of me. I suffer for the sake of someone else. The true test is when I'm in a hurry. When I'm in the drive-thru at any fast food restaurant, I always pay for the customer behind me no matter the cost of their order. I always notice the cashier is shocked when I volunteer to do that. The cashier looks at me like, "Are you serious?" And I smile with a big yes because I want to give to others when they least expect it. I always tell the cashier to tell the recipient, "May God bless you." The customers behind me may not see my giving as suffering, but I do because it's not something I have to do. I choose to do it. So as you see, you can use your time and resources to suffer for the sake of others. Yes, I'm busy, and I always have things to do. Yes, I have bills, and I'm trying to provide for my home, but I can still give my time and resources. And as long as you're thinking about others, you definitely won't have time to judge them because you will make other people matter and not yourself. Madea would say, "Love people and not things and use things and not people." That is one of her many mottos that I've incorporated into my life. I believe you must suffer before you can risk doing what you love. I love people, so I believe it's important for me to suffer. One thing I've learned is that the more you try to avoid suffering, the more you suffer because smaller and more insignificant things begin to torture you in proportion to your fear of being hurt. I'm just fortunate enough to understand this now in life rather than later because I understand putting others first.

So, we all have different tipping points because we are all different in some way, but we are all trying to take that next step in life. Whether it's a father trying to provide for his family, a mother spending the last of her paycheck to clothe her children, or a quadriplegic getting out of bed each day with the help of an aide, we all have different steps we are taking. Just know that there's a tipping point and that you have the power and ability to influence others in a good or bad way. How is that possible? Well, remember the concepts of the Law of the Few, the Stickiness Factor, and the Power of Context. You may be one of the few people that have the power to influence others to do the right or wrong thing. Others may have the stickiness factor to what you say and do because of the confidence others have in you. No matter the context of what you say and do, it can be perceived as correct if others see you do certain things. Never underestimate your ability to influence others. So I share my tipping point to help others deal with their own. In helping other people, I've also learned that I help myself. And last but not least, consider your vision and learn how to make people matter. Just know that if the vision you have for your life, your job, your family, and so on, doesn't include helping others or getting help from others then it is not big enough. And the best way to learn how to make people matter is to serve them. You must first know the people you are serving and learn how to meet their needs. Once that is assured, learn how to suffer for the sake of others. Even though we all have different titles such as brother, sister, mother, father, we all can become as one when we become a servant. So to tip the scales with our next steps, we need to become like Christ, who was a servant to all no matter what this world offered him.

Complete the Chapter Review below. Record and date your responses in a journal or composition notebook.

CHAPTER REVIEW

1. Identify the most important people on your team. (Personal, professional, etc..)

2. What is your tipping point? (the one thing that you need help to overcome)

3. How can you use your tipping in order to help those around you?

CHAPTER 9

IT NEVER GETS EASIER, YOU JUST GET STRONGER

All the adversity I've had in my life, all my troubles and obstacles have strengthened me. You may not realize it when it happens, but a kick in the teeth may be the best thing in the world for you.

—Walt Disney

"If you do it right, you'll do it light. But if you do it wrong, you'll do it long." Those were the words of my strength and conditioning coach when I played basketball. I've always wondered why so many people have a hard time doing things the right way. I've learned that if you do things the right way, it will not be that hard and you'll get stronger. But if you do things the wrong way, it will take longer than you planned.

I can really appreciate things in life now because I know life does not get easier, we just get stronger in order to deal with what life has to offer. At least, we all should strive to get stronger in whatever we put our hands to. Author Stephen Covey says in his book *The 8th Habit*, "At birth, we are given 'birth gifts,' talents, privileges, and opportunities that would remain unopened except through our own decision and effort. A baby at birth may be the most dependent creation on earth and yet within a few short years, it can become the most powerful. The more we use and magnify our present talents, the more talents we are given and the greater our capacity becomes."[i] The purpose of this chapter is to remind readers that we are all given the same opportunity, to recognize that life should not get easier but we should get stronger by the way we live through it. I believe Mother Teresa summed it all up:

> Life is an opportunity, benefit from it.
> Life is beauty, admire it.
> Life is bliss, taste it.
> Life is a dream, realize it.
> Life is a challenge, meet it.
> Life is a duty, complete it.
> Life is a game, play it.
> Life is a promise, fulfill it.
> Life is sorrow, overcome it.
> Life is a song, sing it.
> Life is a struggle, accept it.
> Life is a tragedy, confront it.
> Life is an adventure, dare it.

> Life is luck, make it.
> Life is too precious, do not destroy it.
> Life is life, fight for it.
>
> (Mother Teresa, "Life")

Life has continued to teach me lessons, and I'm thankful that I have the desire to not only notice those lessons but except them in my heart. I've been able to discover my voice by understanding a simple concept. That is the concept of "great gifts mean great responsibilities; greater gifts, greater responsibilities." That concept is a summarized version of Luke 12:48. I believe as individuals that we have the freedom to choose responsibilities or we can choose to have a victim mentality and play the blame game. So personally, we can choose our responsibilities because we need to understand that everyone has been given a gift, which is the freedom of choice. We can choose to respond to our responsibilities or we can become a victim and blame someone else. I do understand that we all are hurt at some point in our lives but we must realize we have to move on. Everyone has been hurt by someone; some just decide to let that pain rule their life which keeps them from taking personal responsibility for their own actions. It's not what happens to us…it's how we respond to what happens to us. I truly believe that to whom much is given, whether trials and tribulations or talents and abilities, much will always be required.

How did I learn to accept that concept? I learned this concept by getting an education. Most people think an education is about going to school and getting a degree. I don't see it that way. I see an education as learning as much as you can from every situation you find yourself in. The eccentric psychiatrist R.D. Laing captured it best. He said, "The range of what we think and do is limited by what we fail to notice. And because we fail to notice that we fail to notice, there is little we can do to change; until we notice how failing to notice shapes our thoughts and deeds."[ii]

For example, when I was a freshman in high school, I said I was never going to college after high school. But once I was able to get basketball scholarship offers from different colleges, I realized that going to college was possible. Once I finished college, I said that I was never going back because I only wanted to have a bachelor's degree. After graduating college and playing professional basketball, I realized that I needed to further my education with a master's degree. And after the master's degree, I realized that I needed have a doctorate degree for opportunities for promotion. In all those experiences, I not only learned from the academic standpoint but I learned about other aspects in life. I believe at first that I was very limited in my thinking because I failed to notice how important an education is. And with that kind of thinking, I didn't want to change my attitude towards pursuing an education. But once basketball opportunities forced me to notice what I failed to notice, then I had to notice I needed to change my thoughts and deeds for the future.

So I encourage everyone to take their education seriously, whether you are in school, college, church service, and even on your job. You decide what and if you want to learn and no one else can do it for you. Dr. Martin Luther King summed up the purpose of education in an essay written during his junior year at Morehouse College in 1946. According to King, education must discipline the mind and orient human life around a set of morals. Without this latter component, King warns, education is "a ship without a compass."[iii] In other words, discipline your own mind and learn to live a life around a set of morals. So whether you are in school, at work, or somewhere else, ask yourself, is your education important to you? If so, lead others so they can find their way because it's not enough to know the truth, but we must love the truth and sacrifice for it.

If you are a leader or you plan to be a leader in the future, you might be asking yourself, how do you love the truth and sacrifice for it? Well, you must learn to lead with **SOUL (Sincerity, Optimism, Unity and Love)** in your current capacity. Leadership is not about title or position, but it's about serving others the best way you know how and continuing to learn and grow. Whenever the topic of sincerity comes up, you're always dealing with the impact on human relationships. You can't be sincere without dealing with others. Author John Maxwell says about relationships, "Almost all our sorrows can be traced to relationships with the wrong people and our joys to relationships with the right people."[iv] In either situation, sincerity is what leaves the lasting impression. And I believe once sincerity has left that lasting impression, you'll have credibility with people. I have always wanted to know if the leaders I have followed were honest and sincere with their dealings. Once I realized they were honest and sincere, they had credibility with me in any situation, and that's the type of leader I want to be. I want people to know my convictions and beliefs and I want to connect my hopes, dreams and aspirations to theirs. I realize that if you don't believe in the messenger, then you won't believe in the message so that's why it's important to be sincere in all dealings.

Once you get beyond the sincerity, your insight has to be optimistic at some point. I say at some point because all situations will never be perfect. As leaders, it's important to face the brutal facts but never lose faith. In author Jim Collins' book *Good to Great,* he insists the real question is not, "How do we motivate people? If you have the right people around you, they will be self-motivated. The key is to not de-motivate them. One way to de-motivate people is to ignore the brutal facts of reality."[v] So recognize the facts but act on the implications of those facts. Sometimes facts might say something can't be done but that's why it's important for those that surround you see that you still have faith that anything is possible. There is nothing more joyful than to see someone do something that others say can never be done. That's why I always like to see people redeem themselves after they've made a mistake. It takes determination and drive to confront the brutal facts and act on the implications.

For example, let's take Michael Vick of the Philadelphia Eagles. Here's a guy that had it all. He was third in the Heisman Trophy balloting in college. He left college early to enter the NFL and was drafted first overall by the Atlanta Falcons in 2001. He became the first African-American quarterback to be selected first overall in an NFL draft. In 2007, Vick was implicated in an illegal interstate dog fighting ring in which he pleaded guilty to federal charges and served twenty-one months in prison. He lost his NFL salary and product endorsement deals which lead him to file for bankruptcy in 2008. He was later reinstated to the NFL, he signed with the Philadelphia Eagles, and he was selected to the Pro Bowl in his first season's return. He continues to do community service work to show the humility of his mistakes. He established The Vick Foundation, a nonprofit organization to support at-risk youth and the after school programs that serve them in the Metro Atlanta and Hampton Roads areas and he continues to volunteer at the Humane Society.[vi] I believe

Michael Vick is a great example of recognizing the implications of his mistakes, and I believe he is using it to better those around him. We've all made mistakes but the only difference is that some of our mistakes are highlighted more than others because of fame and status. At the end of the day though, it is my hope that people don't remember the mistakes, I hope people remember the life changing events that may have helped someone else. I like to say that stars shine only when it's dark.

Now, whether you experience failure or success, be sure that unity is the glue that keeps you in contact with those around you that care about you. I believe as leaders it's important to care about people so people will care about you. The story about Pastor Martin Niemoller is a great example about caring about people. "First they came . . ." is a famous statement attributed to Niemoller about the inactivity of German intellectuals following the Nazi rise to power and the purging of their chosen targeted groups. The text of the quotation is usually presented roughly as follows:

They came for the socialist,

and I did not speak up because I was not a socialist.

Then they came for the trade unionists,

and I did not speak up because I was not a trade unionist.

Then they came for the Jews,

and I did not speak up because I was not a Jew.

Then they came for me,

and there was no one left to speak for me.

Niemoller was a German minister who supported Hitler's rise to power at first but when Hitler insisted on the supremacy of the state over religion, he opposed him and his power. This is a perfect example of why it's important to be unified with people. I believe there are times when you will be requested to be unified with people and other times when you are required to be unified. No matter the case, if you don't speak up for others then there will be no one left to speak up for you.

The last component of leading with SOUL is love. I believe the apostle Paul said it best in 1 Corinthians 13:1-3:

> If I could speak all the languages of earth and of angels, but didn't love others, I would only be a noisy gong or a clanging cymbal. If I had the gift of prophecy, and if I understood all of God's secret plans and possessed all knowledge, and if I had such faith that I could move mountains, but didn't love others, I would be nothing. If I gave everything I have to the poor and even sacrificed my body, I could boast about it; but if I didn't love others, I would have gained nothing.[vii]

My grandmother always had a way of sharing her wisdom, most of which came from the Bible. She would tell me that money is not everything but to try to work honestly to get it. She would tell me that it's OK to have nice clothes, car, and house but to realize those things never show who I am. I remember her telling me to love people and not things but to use things and not people. And if you really think about it, the things you don't enjoy are often the things you're not good at and the things you're good at, you really enjoy doing them.

I find it amazing that I can remember all those things now that I'm adult. I wish I could have just had a tape recorder to listen to her sharing her insight and her laughter. I'm just thankful that I've been able to retain so much of her insights and wisdom that she passed on to me. My hope is that the more I continue to try to be a better person, the more I will recall of what she shared with me. There's an old adage that says, "If you want one year of success, grow grain. If you want ten years of success, grow trees, but if you want a hundred years of prosperity, grow people." So I hope this book will help people grow to be their best.

As we all get older, more mature, and hopefully wiser with each breath, realize that life should not get any easier based on what we deal with or go through. But you should get stronger each day based on your beliefs. I hope this chapter helped you realize that life is a precious gift that's given by God. We are charged to do our best each day. First, remember that great gifts mean great responsibilities, and greater gifts require greater responsibilities. I believe

I'm more talented than others in certain ways, and I believe others are more talented than me in many ways. The point of recognizing that is not for me to be in competition with others but for me to realize that I have a special place in this world and others also have their special place. The key is to understand what gifts you have and be sure you apply them as best as possible and also to allow others to help you based on their own gifts.

Secondly, realize that your education should be important to you no matter what stage you are in life. I consider myself a lifelong learner because even with all my life experiences, I've been able to learn something continuously no matter the outcome. There's an old adage that says, "A man who has a bull by the tail knows five or six things more than someone who never touched a bull." In other words, nothing beats experience so continue to learn and don't forget the lessons. And then take it one step further and share those experiences with others so they may learn from them and grow.

And last but not least, learn to lead with SOUL in whatever capacity you currently serve. My leadership is all about Sincerity, Optimism, Unity and Love (SOUL). I believe you have to take a self evaluation in order to believe in yourself and open up to hearing the leadership call. I've been able to open myself up to making a difference by learning to be sincere in all dealings, learning to have optimism even when it looks like everything is going against me, learning to be unified with people even when it looks like there is no agreement, and then learning to love myself and then pass that love on to others. I've always believe that you can't give something you don't have so you have to love yourself first. I believe author Marianne Williamson sums it up with an excerpt known as "Our deepest fear":

> Our deepest fear is not that we are inadequate. Our deepest fear is that we are powerful beyond measure. It is our light, not our darkness that most frightens us. We ask ourselves, Who am I to be brilliant, gorgeous, talented, fabulous? Actually, who are you *not* to be? You are a child of God. Your playing small does not serve the world. There's nothing enlightened about shrinking so that other people won't feel insecure around you. We are all meant to shine, as children do. We were born to make manifest the glory of God that is within us. It's not just in some of us; it's in everyone. And as we let our own light shine, we unconsciously give other people permission to do the same. As we're liberated from our own fear, our presence automatically liberates others.[viii]

Chapter 10

The Enduring Legacy

I don't want to lose my name because that's how I know myself. Whether you know it or not, there is a legacy here.

—Dr. Samuel Jones

When I think about the word legacy, the first thing that comes to mind is leaving something behind for someone else. In this chapter, I want you to think about what you will leave behind for the next generation. I will share a few thought-provoking examples of how other people's legacies made an impact on my life. I want this book to represent a small portion of my legacy and what I would like to leave behind for others.

What if you became famous, or infamous, for doing something others thought was evil? Would their thoughts of you make you change your outlook on your legacy? Or better yet, what if you read your obituary in the newspaper, online, or heard it on the news on the television? Would those things make you think about what kind of legacy you were leaving behind? Well, that actually happened, and it gave someone a new cause for giving hope to other people.

Alfred Bernhard Nobel was a Swedish chemist, engineer, innovator, and armaments manufacturer who invented dynamite, among other things. Nobel held 355 different patents, of which dynamite was the most well-known. In 1888, Alfred's brother Ludvig Nobel died, and a French newspaper mistakenly published Alfred's obituary. The obituary condemned him for his invention of dynamite and is said to have brought about his decision to leave a better legacy after his death. The obituary stated, "Le Marchand de la mort est mort," (The merchant of death is dead) and went on to say, "Dr. Alfred Nobel, who became rich by finding ways to kill more people faster than ever before, died yesterday." Alfred was disappointed with what he read and became concerned with how he would be remembered. On November 27, 1895, at the Swedish-Norwegian Club in Paris, Nobel signed his last will and testament and set aside the bulk of his estate to establish the Nobel Prize, to be awarded annually without distinction of nationality. After his death a little more than a year later, this amounted to an estimated $250 million. Five awards are given annually. One award is given in the areas of physical science, chemistry, and in medical science or physiology. The fourth is for literary work "in an ideal direction," and the fifth is to be given to the person or society that renders the greatest service to the cause of international diplomacy. Today, the award is better known as the Nobel Peace Prize and is easily seen as the highest award given and is known worldwide. Nobel is now remembered for the prize and not for his work with dynamite. He was able to influence his legacy by considering his impact on society, which lead to an enduring legacy.

What if you were to be the inducted into a Hall of Fame, who would you thank and why? One particular Basketball Hall of Fame speech not only inspired me, but it lifted my spirits. David Robinson, better known as "the Admiral," thanked everyone who made him who he is on and off the court like most inductees. But what caught my attention was how he spoke directly to his family, more importantly, how he used that once-in-a-lifetime moment to speak of life, hope, and dreams to his three sons. He called each one of them by name and spoke to them as though they were the only ones in the room. He spoke passionately:

First, David Jr., I'm really proud of you. I hope this gives you something you want to live up to and to be proud of the Robinson name. You're so intelligent and so wonderful, and I want to say I love you. Next, to Cory, you're multitalented, a young man after God's own heart, and I love you. And to my son Justin, the youngest who is my heart, who's always on my lap and hanging on my neck. You're brilliant and exciting and a natural born leader. I'm proud of each one of you guys, and I hope this makes you want to carry out the Robinson name.

I like the fact that he used this platform to speak his hopes and dreams to his young men. He focused on the concept of making sure they remember the Robinson name will always be bigger than they are, but to also help them realize that they are a part of something special. By being a part of something special, his sons have a responsibility to be productive citizens in society and hopefully will add to the enduring legacy of the Robinson family.

Another great example of legacy comes from one of my favorite Disney movies The Lion King. In the scene, King Mufasa has a conversation with his cub son Simba on the top of Pride Mountain overlooking the kingdom:

Mufasa: Look, Simba. Everything the light touches is our kingdom.

Simba: Wow!

Mufasa: A king's time as ruler rises and falls like the sun. One day, Simba, the sun will set on my time here and will rise with you as the new king.

Simba: And this will be all mine?

Mufasa: Everything.

Simba: Everything the light touches. What about that shadowy place?

Mufasa: That's beyond our borders. You must never go there, Simba.

Simba: But I thought a king can do whatever he wants.

Mufasa: Oh, there's more to being king than . . . getting your way all the time.

(Mufasa starts back down the rock)

Simba: (Awed) There's more?

Mufasa: (Chuckles) Simba . . . Everything you see exists together, in a delicate balance. As king, you need to understand that balance and respect all the creatures—from the crawling ant to the leaping antelope.

Simba: But, Dad, don't we eat the antelope?

Mufasa: Yes, Simba, but let me explain. When we die, our bodies become the grass. And the antelope eat the grass. And so we are all connected in the great Circle of Life.

   The Lion King is a great movie about legacy because of two important facts. First, Mufasa showed the importance that as king, you have to understand that "a king's time rises and falls like the sun." It doesn't matter what position we currently have; it's important to realize that one day we will no longer be here. Even our time as human beings is limited. So always remember that and do the best with the time you have. And second, this is an important movie about legacy because it showed the importance of how all living creatures are connected in the great circle of life. Mufasa explained how there is a delicate balance that the king must understand and respect. I believe as humans, we must all try to understand and respect all people because of our differences. If we truly think about it, there is a need for all people no matter the race, nationality, etc. Whenever the balance is off center or out of whack, that is when we stop caring about each other. Of course, this movie had several more teachable moments, but this particular scene with Mufasa and Simba seemed to inspire and motive me to care more about people in ways I never imagined. I hope it did the same for you.

Now even as inspiring as the examples of Alfred Nobel, David Robinson, and Mufasa and Simba are, the next story is one that touched my heart the moment I heard it. This particular story is the one that encouraged me to write this chapter and title it "The Enduring Legacy." I call this story "The Responsibility of Leaving a Legacy" because it can change a life.

The story begins at an agricultural high school in Southern Mississippi. In the 1920s in Mississippi, most high schools were considered agricultural high schools because the students lived on campus and they had cattle and they raised their own vegetables, etc. Since the students lived on campus, they had access to a chapel on campus for their worship services. During that time, a student named Tom, who was about eighteen, was the minister who conducted the services. And like all other students on campus, the football players participated in worship services. But there was one player, by the name of Jimmy, who always came to service but was never interested in what was going on. Tom insisted that Jimmy always had a bad attitude towards worship service, the minister's messages, and people in general. When Tom first shared this story, he insisted that he had given up on Jimmy back in school.

Well, some fifty years later, Tom comes back to the town where had he preached his last sermon on that campus. Since then, a lot of things have changed on that campus and in that small town. Today, that small agricultural high school is now a thriving junior college in the heart of Jones County, Mississippi. The agricultural high school started with about thirty students. Today, Jones County Junior College has an average enrollment of about forty-five hundred students. Well, Tom comes back to campus for a fifty-year class reunion to visit with classmates, and he is amazed to see how the campus has changed. When he gets to town, he checks in at the Alice Hotel, a small local bed and breakfast. Tom remembers the Alice Hotel from fifty years ago. As Tom checks in, the clerk at the desk makes a dramatic scene which neither she nor Tom will ever forget. As Tom gives his reservation and check-in information, she asks, "Are you Tom——?" He maintains, "Yes, that's me." With a sigh of disbelief, the clerk asks him again, "Are you Tom——?" Now Tom is thinking, "What is wrong with this young lady? Did I do something wrong or did someone steal my identity?" All of these thoughts are running through Tom's head at that moment. He declares yes again. Then the clerk again with a big heave and sigh asks, "Are you Tom——?" Immediately, Tom says, "Yes, I'm very sure I am." All of a sudden, the clerk is now overwhelmed with tears and excitement. At this point, Tom is very confused and unsure as to how to respond. He's not sure if he should try to calm her, call for emergency help or to just ease out the building. Instead, Tom stands there patiently waiting for the clerk to gather her emotions. He said it seemed like five minutes had passed as all of this was happening. Finally, the clerk says with a big smile and tears in her eyes, "You are Tom——; you were a classmate of my grandfather Jimmy——. You were also my grandfather's minister while you all were in high school. My grandfather got saved while listening to your last message in the chapel on campus. The title of your last sermon was 'There is plenty of work to be done.' My grandfather told me this before he passed away several years ago." The clerk said, "I never thought in a million years that I would ever meet you." Immediately after the clerk finished her story, tears began to roll from Tom's eyes. Now the roles had been reversed. In his heart, Tom realized that sometimes we give up on people when we try to help them, but he learned that God does not give up on us. He was convinced that God's grace and mercy allowed Jimmy to be saved. It allowed Jimmy to share his life-changing experience with his granddaughter. It allowed his granddaughter the opportunity to meet the man who preached a saving message to her grandfather, and it allowed the preacher to hear some fifty years later that a person he never thought would change his life got saved. This is what an enduring legacy is all about.

As I bring this chapter to an end, think of the examples I've given. Think about reading your obituary in the newspaper. How would it read if written today? What lasting impression would you leave upon your friends, family, or strangers that you came in contact with? How will the next stranger see you? Or what if you were inducted into a Hall of Fame, who would you thank and why? Would you share that famous stage with others? How would you plant seeds of life, hope, and inspiration into those that you love? How would your speech impact that stranger who never met you? Or what if you were King for a Day? How would you use your throne? How would you use your power and authority? How would you impart wisdom to the next king in line? How would you treat that stranger who could do nothing for you? Or what if you were able to see someone change their life because of something you said or did for them? Are you doing things now to benefit others in a way that they can say that you lead them to believe in Christ?

I asked myself those same questions once I began writing my book. They are questions I asked myself once I started writing, and I will continue to ask myself once this book is completed. My thoughts have always been to think about MY legacy because I had to overcome so much. The main thing I want you, the reader, to gain from this book is to remember you will leave a legacy when you are gone. The thing is, though, will that legacy live through the lives of others? In other words, will they want to make this world a better place because they saw how you lived your life? I understand that no one is perfect, but we should strive to be better people each day. I've had ups and downs and turnarounds, but I never gave up because I was introduced to a stranger. That stranger was Jesus Christ., I knew I was introduced to him when I was young, but I didn't acknowledge who he was. I didn't accept him because I didn't quite understand the true meaning of accepting Jesus. Madea would always say, "Just keep living, you'll understand one day. Jesus is the truth…the light…the love that we all seek. He died for you, and he is in you. Don't ever lose sight of that." Once I accepted him, then I realized that I needed to change my life. And to be honest, accepting Christ into my life was similar to the lesson in one of my favorite books, The Precious Present, by

Spencer Johnson. It's a story that takes about an hour to read, but it can change your perspective on life.

To highlight the book, an old man is on his porch watching as young boy plays and does his chores with a very happy and carefree attitude. The boy eventually got to know the old man, and the boy tried to learn about the "Precious Present." The man explained, "It is a present because it is a gift. And it is precious because anyone who receives such a present is happy forever."

"Wow!" the little boy exclaimed. "I hope someone gives me the Precious Present. Maybe I'll get it for Christmas." The boy didn't quite understand what it actually could be that could keep him happy forever. Each time the time boy guessed, the man said no. The old man said, "The richness is rare, indeed, but the wealth of the Present comes only from itself." As the boy grew into a young man, he kept trying to find what the Precious Present was. The harder he tried to find out what the Present was, the unhappier and more frustrated he became. "I'm afraid you don't understand," the old man responded. "You already know what the Precious Present is. You already know where to find it. And you already know how it can make you happy. You knew it best when you were a small child. You simply have forgotten."

The unhappy man, like many of us, grew tired of looking for the Precious Present. Most of the time, we try to find the precious present or happiness in material things or accomplishments. That's not to say that those things are bad, it's just that those things can keep you out of balance if you don't have your priorities in order. So many people grow tired of chasing those simple dreams and aspirations that when they don't achieve them, they stop trying. And most of the time, it eventually happens just like it happened to this unhappy man. Sometimes it takes an inventory evaluation to realize that the Precious Present is just that: **THE PRESENT.** Not the past, and not the future, but **THE PRECIOUS PRESENT.** So for me, the Precious Present was always my personal experience with Christ even though I didn't recognize it at the time. All those times Madea talked to me about reading my Bible, going to church, and trying to find my purpose in life, she was trying to introduce me to the **PRECIOUS PRESENT.** As I reflect on my experiences I've written about in this book, I've come to realize that I've had the **PRECIOUS PRESENT** all along. The past is history, the future is a mystery, but the present is just that, a present. I realize that we are all given precious moments on earth for a reason. I want my legacy to be that I not only enjoyed life but that I helped others succeed in trying to find the **PRECIOUS PRESENT.** I want others to feel the same joy I have in knowing Christ and living a life of value and servanthood. I hope this chapter will encourage you to think about how your legacy can be enduring once you are gone. But while you are here now, you still have the Precious Present of the current moment. The only way your legacy can be enduring is if you have Christ at the center of it.

Complete the Chapter Review below. Record and date your responses in a journal or composition notebook.

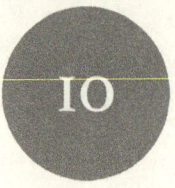

CHAPTER REVIEW

1. What do you want your legacy to be? (Personal/professional)

2. Name at least 3 things that you can to support, fulfill your legacy.

3. Name one thing that you will do each day to support & fulfill your legacy.

CHAPTER 11

THE MAN I KNOW NOW

It's not who you are that holds you back, it's who you think you're not.
—Author Unknown

As you've read through this book, I expect you have some idea of the man I never knew. If you're still wondering, the man I never knew is actually a compilation of the understanding of three individuals: my biological father, my Lord and Savior Jesus Christ, and the person I am today. Writing this book has allowed me to release my emotions in a way I never dreamed. I've always known that adversity could bring out the best or worst in a person, depending on the choices made. While I haven't always made the right choices, I'm glad I've been able to deal with the pain and frustration that came with my experiences. With each experience, I've been privileged to learn more about who I am yet becoming today.

Chapter 1: Exposure Leads to Experience

If I'm going to learn and grow, I must know what questions to ask myself and how to apply those answers to my life. That's what I thought about when I first decided to write this book. I've been exposed to so many opportunities that I wouldn't have had the chance to pursue if it wasn't for the influence of my grandmother, my ability to play basketball, and so many other opportunities that I did not mention. I've been able to graduate from college with a bachelor's degree for which I was given a scholarship. I've been able to travel to and live in a foreign country for a year playing the sport I love. I've been exposed to the education system where I was encouraged to pursue a higher level of education. Not only that, I'm now in a position to help students pursue their dreams and aspirations. All of those things have allowed me to experience life in a way I never deemed possible. That's one reason why I wanted to write this book. It was my hope to give you a taste of my experiences to help you along your journey. This book has helped me see the big picture in my thinking and my actions because my world has been expanded. I've been able to stir up the memories of the time spent with my grandmother and numerous other experiences that have been buried deep within my soul. I feel a sense of freedom now that I have my thoughts on paper.

The Man I Never Knew   Samuel L. Jones, Ph.D.

It is also my hope that I learn from every experience in my life. Even though I've had some success so far, it is no time to rest. I want to stay teachable and stay hungry. I always believed I had my Ph.D. before I earned my Ph.D. from Mississippi State University. I always knew to Play Hard Daily no matter what I was doing, whether that was on the basketball court or in the classroom. I knew I was not the sharpest knife in the drawer, so I always had to work hard. I believe my ability to work hard always gave me permission to go in different directions, to break new ground, or to find new and different things to accomplish. I also knew that just because I played hard and gave it my best, I would not always be successful or get the desired results.

For example, my freshman year at USM, I played against the best college basketball player who came through the University of Memphis. His name is Anfernee "Penny" Hardaway. This was our first conference game that season, and I was asked to guard him based on our scouting report. Hardaway was a sophomore standing six foot seven weighing about 215 pounds, and I was a freshman standing six foot four weighing about 175 pounds soaking wet. As you can see, I was a major underdog, but that didn't discourage me from playing my heart out. At the time, I thought that if I played hard 100 percent of the time I was on the floor, I could stop him. I played my heart out, and we lost the game. I held him to twenty-eight points, ten rebounds, and twelve assists. For those of you not familiar with basketball, twenty-eight points, ten rebounds, and twelve assists is something called a "triple double." That's like an individual scoring five touchdowns in football, hitting for the cycle in baseball, or scoring ten goals in soccer. This experience taught me that even though I might play hard, it won't always guarantee the results I desire. It did guarantee me that I gave my all, and I was able to live with the results. You might wonder whatever happened to Penny Hardaway. Well, he went on to play thirteen seasons in the NBA, and he was the MVP of the Rookie All-Star game. He also won a gold medal as a member of the USA men's basketball team in the 1996 summer Olympics, and he would have six career triple-doubles in the NBA. Based on his resume, it was an honor have played against a special and talented athlete like him. One thing I learned was that my exposure to playing against Penny Hardaway led to an experience that I'll never forget. That experience allows me to understand that there will always be more opportunities out there in the world to gain knowledge. As long as you are exposed to challenges, you will experience exactly what you need in every situation, so it helps to be led by the spirit.

Proverbs 16:9: A person may plan his own journey, but the Lord directs his steps.

Chapter 2: Learning to Lead as Others Laugh

When was the last time you laughed with someone else at your own expense? Maybe you haven't thought about that. It might not be easy, but if you try hard enough, you can find something good in the midst of the most difficult, uncomfortable situations. I believe that it's easy for individuals to take themselves too seriously. I've been fortunate enough to learn to laugh at myself and always to realize that it's not that serious. In Laugh Again by Chuck Swindoll, he explains that when Mother Teresa was asked what the requirements were for anyone wanting to help her in the grimy streets and narrow alleys of Calcutta, she cited two things: the desire to work hard and a joyful attitude. If you think about it, those are requirements everyone should have for every task. I just shared above about how I had my PHD (Play Hard Daily), but I like the idea of a joyful attitude. There's no better way to have a joyful attitude than by learning to laugh at yourself. I've learned that if you can laugh at yourself, you'll probably experience less tension, less stress, and you'll probably be healthier. Laughing at myself helps me keep things in their proper perspective, and it helps me not to take myself too seriously.

Before my dunking incident at USM, I was highly sensitive and sort of insecure. Looking back now, I believe this incident helped me to grow up and become secure about who I am. Once I began to laugh about this incident, I realized that it takes great confidence to laugh at myself. Compared to my simple basketball experience, one of the most touching instances of humor I've come across is in Viktor Frankl's deeply moving book, Man's Search for Meaning. This book chronicles his experiences as a concentration camp inmate. In this book, he describes his method of finding a reason to live. Frankl insisted that sometimes men in the camp would create dreams about future dinner engagements that they might forget themselves when the soup was served. In their imaginings, they would pretend they were at a fancy party, and the servers at the concentration camp were the hostesses. The men would beg the hostesses to scoop the soup "from the bottom" because the odds were better they might get a rare pea or piece of carrot. These dreams were created to imagine themselves outside the camp even though they were living in hell. This was an attempt to develop a sense of humor and see things in a humorous light while mastering the art of living. Their situation was certainly nothing to joke about, but Frankl observed that the people who would survive fought to retain as much of their personality as possible, including their sense of humor. I believe that when you laugh at yourself or keep a joyful attitude, you allow yourself to open a safety valve to be released from your present troubles. Eventually, you'll remind yourself that there's nothing to laugh about now but in ten years, you'll be able to smile at the courage you showed in your time of great adversity. Always know there is a reason for optimism.

Proverbs 17:22: A joyful heart is good medicine, but depression drains one's strength.

Chapter 3: The Truth is The Truth

I like what philosopher, art critic, and writer Denis Diderot says about the truth. He insists that "we swallow greedily any lie that flatters us, but we sip only little by little at a truth we find bitter." I can definitely relate to swallowing lies that flatter, but sipping only a little of the truth. As I've shared, the truth is the truth. One thing I've learned about the truth is that it really means nothing if you just know it and recognize it. I've learned that the truth really means something when you live it out in your life. Will you be perfect? No. Just because you are not perfect doesn't mean you shouldn't strive to live a life without regrets. When you strive to live a life without regrets, you at least acknowledge and recognize what the truth means. When I didn't acknowledge or recognize what the truth meant, I didn't care how I lived. I'm just thankful I've been given at least 13,140 days, 315,360 hours, 18,921,600 seconds or 36 years to live a better life. I'm thankful that my clock is still ticking. All in all, whether we live by it or die by it, the truth will always stand, so it's always important to give it much thought.

Haggai 1:7: Carefully consider your ways!

Chapter 4: Success by Choice, Not by Chance

The chapter on success by choice can best be summed up with one of the famous quotes of American poet and essayist Ralph Waldo Emerson: "To laugh often and much; to win the respect of intelligent people and the affection of children . . . to leave the world a better place . . . to know even one life has breathed easier because you have lived. This is to have succeeded." I've always wanted to inspire those who have no hope and to find the best in people who some may deem as worthless. I hope this chapter provided a road map to choose success. There is one thing I always will remember about choosing success, and that is to remember that success and failure go hand in hand. It is nearly impossible to have one without the other. Failure will always remind you that you can still be successful, but you must be humble enough to recognize the areas you need to improve upon. Success will always remind you that you can still fail. You will continue to have a target on your back as long as you're successful. I'm afraid that so many people give up just at the thought of failure. I say quitters never win, and winners never quit. Continue to take chances in life to choose success. Always remember that you will create your future by your current decisions.

1 Corinthians 9:24: Don't you realize that everyone who runs in a race runs to win, but only one runner gets the prize? Run like them, so that you can win.

Chapter 5: Change is Scary, But it's Good!

Writing this book has allowed me to do some reflective thinking, during which I've gained a true perspective as to why I viewed change as so scary before. Now, I know that change is important and good for me. The first thing I've been able to do is to reflect back and recapture some of my experiences to evaluate them. For the past twenty-five years, I believe I distanced myself from those experiences, and I was not able to see them with a fresh set of eyes. The process of writing a book has allowed me to get beyond the surface of my emotions and feelings to dig deep into the depth of my soul to get rid of some of the emotional baggage that I was carrying around. It is my goal to turn those memorable life experiences into valuable life lessons so that others can possibly understand their life experiences. English playwright and poet John Heywood says, "If you will call your troubles experiences and remember that every experience develops some latent force within you, you will grow vigorous and happy, however adverse your circumstances may seem to be." I believe that experience is what you got by not having it when you needed it.

I tell my college students that if you don't value your current experiences, you will continue to be shocked and surprised in life because you didn't pay attention to your past experiences. My hope for my readers is that this book will help them realize they need to change and continue to grow as individuals. I've been told that inch by inch change is a cinch, but yard by yard, change is hard. I've tried to change things in my life overnight, but I soon realized that it takes time for anything to change. I've learned to give myself room to grow and to improve in the areas that I need to. I'm always reminded to have enough joy to make me pleasant to be around, to remember my trials that I've experienced to make me strong, to know that there is already enough sorrow in the world to keep me human, and to always keep enough hope to keep me happy and humble. Even though change is scary, I've been able to realize that it's good for me, and I hope you feel the same.

Hebrews 12:11: We don't enjoy being disciplined. It always seems to cause more pain than joy. But later on, those who learn from that discipline have peace that comes from doing what is right.

Chapter 6: OK! means Opportunity Knocking

Technology can be your best friend or your worst enemy. That's what I always say whenever I'm exposed to something new dealing with technology. With that said, I have to realize that being exposed to new technology is just another opportunity knocking. Of course, technology is just an example so you can change that to new people you're meeting, new places you're going, or even a new food you're trying for the first time. I've had to discipline myself to no become complacent with what I already know. I've also learned to recognize opportunities knocking by discernment. One way I do that is to listen intently to others who have more experience than me. As author Kenneth Wells says, "A good listener tries to understand thoroughly what the other person is saying. In the end, he may disagree sharply, but before he disagrees, he wants to know exactly what it is he is disagreeing with." Discipline and discernment have allowed me to recognize the opportunities knocking around me by helping me to learn from my experiences and to learn from others' experiences.

Psalm 27:11: Teach me your way, O Lord; lead me in a straight path.

Chapter 7: The Making of a Champion: From Inspiration to Application

The making of a champion has to start somewhere. I've learned that it takes things happening in your life to get your attention before you can recognize what exactly to do next. You have to be inspired before you can apply yourself. Like Muhammad Ali, sometimes that inspiration may come at the most unexpected time in your life. I've learned that going from inspiration to application MUST start with your thinking. As an individual, you are charged with creating your success. My father-in-law likes to say, "The choices you make determine the future that you create." Most people find a reason why something can't be done, but it takes inspiration and application to be the one to find a reason why something can be done. In other words, you have to be the one to make today count for the sake of tomorrow by learning from yesterday.

Ecclesiastes 11:4: Whoever watches the wind will never plant. Whoever looks at the clouds will never harvest.

Chapter 8: Your Tipping Point is Your Next Step

My tipping point is always my next step because I've learned how to deal with setbacks in my life. This chapter helped me to revisit the past to gain a true perspective and think with better clarity and understanding. I understand that my spiritual life should be the foundation for everything I believe and act upon. I'm glad that I've been able to use the adversity in my life to possibly help and encourage someone else. I believe everyone has adversity in life, but the difference is how you get through it. Hopefully, you endure in a way that will help someone else. For that reason, the ideals and events in this chapter on tipping points have turned my experience into insight because I know who to turn to for all the answers I will ever need.

Psalm 6:9: The Lord has heard my plea for mercy. The Lord accepts my prayer.

Chapter 9: It Never gets Easier, You Just Get Stronger

I've learned that I can't commit to something that isn't important to me, and I can't commit to something that doesn't fit with who I am and how I see myself. I've learned to define my values and principles which have allowed me to set expectations for my life. I had to realize that headaches, pains, misunderstandings, and disappointments are a part of life, but it's all in how I deal with it. My ultimate success depends on how well I know myself, what I value, and why I value it. The better I know who I am and what I believe in, the better I am at making sense of the conflicting demands that I get daily. Ralph Waldo Emerson says, "What lies behind us and what lies before us are tiny matters compared to what lies within us." In the end, I know that I don't get physically stronger but what I believe in and what is in me gets stronger, and that is what gets me through adversity.

2 Corinthians 5:17: Whoever is a believer in Christ is a new creation. The old way of living has disappeared. A new way of living has come into existence.

Chapter 10: The Enduring Legacy

What preparations should you make now to have an enduring legacy? Well, what you leave behind is important, whether you give it any thought or not. Your legacy will always outlive you. The thing about making preparations is that we all have the same chance and a choice to determine what legacy to leave. A proverb says, "By bravely enduring it, an evil which cannot be avoided is overcome." I've learned that most of the time, everyone has some type of evil to deal with but it has to be recognized to be overcome. I've learned that the only way to overcome any evil is with good, as Alfred Nobel overcame the evils of dynamite by establishing the Nobel Prize. You must start with yourself to know what it is you want as your enduring legacy, particularly if that legacy is to be a positive one. How do you do that? I believe there are two ways you can have an enduring legacy. The first is to have Christ as the center of your life and learn how to give. I believe that giving is the highest form of living for Christ. Radio personality Paul Harvey said, "If you don't live it, you don't believe it." Without Christ as your center, your life will be consistently centered around decisions based on what you can see physically and not spiritually and you will become an ungrateful person. For example, you might need to have certain things in life to consider yourself successful (money, cars, fame, etc.). I'm thankful that I was taught that none of those things make me the person that I am. I appreciate the fact that love is the most important component of success. If you can love yourself, only then can you learn how to love others. Secondly, it's important to be grateful for what you have and your life experiences. Author H. Jackson Brown reminds us to "remember that everyone you meet is afraid of something, loves something, and has lost something." I believe that when you are grateful, you will realize the importance of other peoples' experience of being afraid, others' experience of loving something, and their experience of losing something. And when you respect other people's experiences, it will help you focus on what needs to change in your life so that you can be a positive influence for others in need.

1 Corinthians 13 1:3: If I could speak all the languages of earth and of angels, but didn't love others, I would only be a noisy gong or a clanging cymbal. If I had the gift of prophecy, and if I understood all of God's secret plans and possessed all knowledge, and if I had such faith that I could move mountains, but didn't love others, I would be nothing. If I gave everything I have to the poor and even sacrificed my body, I could boast about it; but if I didn't love others, I would have gained nothing.

Bonus Chapter: The Man I Know Now

And now that I have my thoughts in this book, I should enjoy the fruits of my labor right? I don't think so. I think I need to enjoy it for what it is and move to the next challenge in my life. As of this moment, I really have no idea what that challenge is. I do know that I want to continue to help people in whatever capacity that may be.

Remember those three individuals who I referred to as the man I never knew (my biological father, my Lord and Savior Jesus Christ, and the person that I am today)? I'm glad that I've been able to share my life experiences concerning all three because it has helped me become a better person. I believe I've been able to understand who I am by sharing my personal experience. My faith has helped me to have faith without being critical of other faiths and to do good deeds whenever possible as opposed to morally judging others because I think I have greater insight into the wishes of the Almighty. I just want to be a person with faith. Faith is the substance of things hoped for, the evidence of things not seen. With that said, I've never seen or known my biological father (to my knowledge), and I don't know my future, but it is my hope that whatever the future has in store for me, I still can be an example for others in terms of living through adversity. It is my prayer to fill that void in my life. If that void is never filled with my desires, I know I will continue to become the man I need to be.

Last but not least, I want to end with a story from Luke 17. There were ten men with leprosy who had met Jesus while he was traveling to Jerusalem. Those ten men asked Jesus to have mercy on them. Immediately when Jesus saw them, he told them to show themselves to the priest. As they went, they all were made clean and healed. When one of them saw that he was healed, he turned back and praised God in a loud voice, and he quickly bowed at Jesus' feet and thanked him. Out of the ten men, only one turned to praise and give thanks. The man I know now understands that I need to continue to praise God for everything that has happened in my life. I know that without my faith, I would not have been able to endure the trials and tribulations of the past. I'm thankful that I've been able to grow and express my thoughts in a way to share them with others. I understand that the highest expression of love is to give without expecting and to accept without exceptions. It is my hope that you have received a gift of love by reading the words in this book, and I hope your dreams and aspirations have been fueled because of my experiences. With that said, I know that I still have so much to learn, because the man I never knew said so.

WORKS CITED

Arbinger Institute, *Leadership and Self-Deception: Getting out of the box.* San Francisco: Berrett-Koelhler, 2002.

Collins, Jim. *Good to Great.* New York: Harper Collins, 2001.

Covey, Stephen. The *8th Habit: From Effectiveness to Greatness.* New York: Free Press, 2004.

Frankl, Victor. *Man's Search for Meaning.* New York: Washington Square Press, 1959.

Gladwell, Malcolm. *The Tipping Point: How Little Things Can Make a Big Difference.* New York: Little, Brown, 2000.

Holtz, Lou. *Winning Every Day.* New York: Harper Collins, 1998.

Johnson, Spencer. *The Precious Present.* New York: Knopf Doubleday, 1984.

Kouzes, James M., and Barry Z. Posner. *A Leader's Legacy.* San Francisco: Jossey-Bass, 2006.

Maxwell, John. *How Successful People Think.* New York: Center Street, 2009.

———. *Talent Is Never Enough*. Nashville: Thomas Nelson, 2007.

Meyer, Paul J. *Unlocking Your Legacy: 25 Keys to Success*. Chicago: Moody, 2002.

O'Malley, Michael. *The Wisdom of Bees: What the hive can teach business about Leadership, Efficiency, and Growth*. New York: Penguin, 2010.

Swindoll, Charles. *Laugh Again: Experience Outrageous Joy*. Nashville: W Publishing, 1992.

Williamson, Marianne. *A Return to Love: Reflections on the Principles of "A Course in Miracles."* New York: Harper Collins, 1992.

NOTES

Chapter 1 Exposure leads to experience

[1] "Delta Directions," accessed November 1, 2010, http://www.deltadirections.org/delta_region/delta_history/index.html.
[1] John Vlach, *Shotgun House: An African Architectural Legacy*, accessed on November 1, 2010, quoted quoted in "Shotgun house," *Wikipedia*, accessed November 1, 2010, http://en.wikipedia.org/wiki/Shotgun_house.

Chapter 2 Learning to lead as others laugh

[1] "Richard Bach Quotes," Explore, accessed November 9, 2010, http://www.brainyquote.com/quotes/authors/r/richard_bach_3.html.
[1] "Quotations about Kindness," The Quote Garden, accessed November 1, 2010,
http://www.quotegarden.com/kindness.html.

Chapter 3 The truth is the truth

[1] "The Internet Movie Database," Amazon, accessed November 11, 2010. http://www.imdb.com/title/tt0082158/taglines.
[1] "Patrick Overton quotes," ThinkExist, accessed November 11, 2010, http://thinkexist.com/quotation/when_you_have_come_to_the_edge_of_all_ligh t_that/173385.html.
[1] 1Kings 19:11-12 (New King James Version).
[1] "Bible study lessons," Glen Davis, accessed November 15, 2010, http://www.free-bible-study-lessons.com/faith-quotes.html.
[1] "Leadership Now," M2 Communications, accessed November 27, 2010, http://www.leadershipnow.com/perseverancequotes.html.

Chapter 4 Success by design, not by chance

[1] "League Leaders," MLB Advanced Media, accessed February 13, 2011, http://mlb.mlb.com/stats/historical/leaders.jsp?c_id=mlb&baseballScope=mlb&s tatType= 1&sortByStat=HR&timeFrame=3&timeSubFrame=0.

[1] "Hank Aaron quotes," ThinkExist, accessed February 13, http://thinkexist.com/quotes/hank_aaron/.

[1] "List of National Football League records (individual),"*Wikipedia*, accessed on February 13, 2011, http://en.wikipedia.org/wiki/List_of_National_Football_League_records_(individual).

[1] "List of National Football League passing touchdowns leaders," *Wikipedia*, accessed February 13, 2011, http://en.wikipedia.org/wiki/List_of_National_Football_League_passing_touchdowns_leaders.

[1] "Fumble," *Wikipedia*, accessed February 13, 2011, http://en.wikipedia.org/wiki/Fumble.

[1] "Brett Favre quotes," accessed February 13, 2011, http://thinkexist.com/quotes/brett_favre/2.html.

[1] "Ancient Persian saying Quotes," accessed November 19, 2010, http://www.famousquotesandauthors.com/authors/ancient_persian_saying_quotes.html.

[1] "David Brinkley quotes," accessed November 22, 2010, http://thinkexist.com/quotes/david_brinkley/.

[1] Lou Holt, *Winning Every Day* (New York: Harper Collins, 1998), 160.

[1] "Charles R. Swindoll quotes," accessed November 22, 2010, http://thinkexist.com/quotation/we_cannot_change_our_past-we_can_not_change_the/201798.html.

[1] "Jonathan_Winters," *Wikipedia*, accessed November 19, 2010, http://en.wikipedia.org/wiki/Jonathan_Winters.

[1] "Anatole_France," *Wikipedia*, accessed November 19, 2010, http://en.wikipedia.org/wiki/Anatole_France.

Chapter 5 Change is scary, but it's good!

[1] "Germaine Greer Quotes," Brainyquote, accessed February 15, 2011, http://www.brainyquote.com/quotes/quotes/g/germainegr119612.html.

[1] Michael O'Malley, *The Wisdom of Bees: What the hive can teach business about Leadership, Efficiency, and Growth* (New York: Penguin, 2010), 14.

[1] Biblegateway, accessed November 29, 2010, http://www.biblegateway.com/passage/?search=proverbs%2016&version=GW.

[1] Biblegateway, accessed December 1, 2010, http://www.biblegateway.com/passage/?search=proverbs%2010&version=NIV.

[1] "Charlie Brown,"*Wikipedia,* accessed December 1, 2010, http://en.wikipedia.org/wiki/Charlie_Brown.

[1] John Maxwell, *How Successful People Think* (New York: Center Street, 2009), 27.
[1] The Arbinger Institute, *Leadership and Self-Deception: Getting out of the box* (San Francisco: Berrett-Koehler, 2002), 16.

Chapter 6 OK! means . . . Opportunity Knocking!

[1] Marc Revere, "Leadership Skills: Opportunity's Knocking—Will You Open the Door?," *Fire Rescue Magazine*, July 6, 2010, accessed December 2, 2010, http://www.firefighternation.com/profiles/blogs/leadership-skills-opportunitys.
[1] Ibid.
[1] Paul J. Meyer, *Unlocking Your Legacy: 25 Keys to Success* (Chicago: Moody Publishers, 2002), 106.
[1] Ibid.
[1] Fred Smith, "How I delivered the goods," *Fortune Small Business*, October 2002, accessed December 2, 2010, http://fedex.com/us/about/news/ontherecord/speaker/fredsmith.pdf.
[1] "Elder Richard G. Scott quotes," ThinkExist, accessed January 13, 2011, http://thinkexist.com/quotation/in_quiet_moments_when_you_think_about_it-you/13250.html.
[1] "H. Jackson Brown quotes," Goodreads, accessed January 8, 2011, http://www.goodreads.com/author/quotes/33394.H_Jackson_Brown_Jr_.

Chapter 7 The making of a champion: from inspiration to application

[1] Doug West, "The Making of a Champion," Motivating Moments, April, 6, 2007, accessed January 6, 2011, http://www.motivateus.com/stories/making-champion.htm.
[1] "Muhammad Ali Quotes," Brainyquote, accessed December 21, 2010, http://www.brainyquote.com/quotes/authors/m/muhammad_ali.html#ixzz17eLuaX93.
[1] "The Muhammad Ali Biography," The Biography Channel website, accessed January 6, 2011, http://www.biography.com/articles/Muhammad-Ali-9181165.
[1] "Muhammad Ali Quotes," Brainyquote, accessed December 21, 2010, http://www.brainyquote.com/quotes/authors/m/muhammad_ali.html#ixzz17eLuaX93.

Chapter 8 Your Tipping Point is Your Next Step

[1] Biblegateway, accessed January 7, 2011, http://www.biblegateway.com/passage/?search=Matthew%205&version=NIV.
[1] Malcolm Gladwell, *The Tipping Point: How Little Things Can Make a Big Difference* (New York: Little, Brown, 2000), 30-133.
[1] "Henri Louis Bergson Quotes," Brainyquote, accessed November 25, 2010, http://www.brainyquote.com/quotes/authors/h/henri_louis_bergson.html.
[1] Biblegateway, accessed January 7, 2011, http://www.biblegateway.com/passage/?search=Ephesions%206&version=NIV.
[1] Biblegateway, accessed February 20, 2011, http://www.biblegateway.com/passage/?search=1%20corinthians%2013&version=NIV.
[1] Biblegateway, accessed January 7, 2011, http://www.biblegateway.com/passage/?search=Proverbs%2023:7&version=NIV.
[1] Biblegateway, accessed January 7, 2011, http://www.biblegateway.com/passage/?search=Matthew%207:1&version=NIV.
[1] James M. Kouzes and Barry Z. Posner, *A Leader's Legacy* (San Francisco: Jossey-Bass, 2006), 13.

Chapter 9 It never gets easier, you just get stronger

[1] Stephen Covey, *The 8th Habit: From Effectiveness to Greatness* (New York: Free Press, 2004), 39.
[1] Ibid.
[1] Martin Luther King Jr., "The Purpose of Education," accessed November 23, 2010, http://www.stanford.edu/group/King/liberation_curriculum/pdfs/purposeofeducation.pdf.
[1] John Maxwell, *Talent Is Never Enough* (Nashville: Thomas Nelson, 2007), 215.
[1] Jim Collins, *Good to Great* (New York: Harper Collins, 2001), 89.
[1] "Michael Vick," *Wikipedia*, accessed February 6, 2011, http://en.wikipedia.org/wiki/Michael_Vick.
[1] Biblegateway, accessed January 9, 2011, http://www.biblegateway.com/passage/?search=1%20Corinthians%2013&version=NLT.
[1] Marianne Williamson, *A Return to Love: Reflections on the Principles of "A Course in Miracles"* (New York: Harper Collins, 1992), 165.

Chapter 10 The enduring legacy . . .

¹ "Alfred Nobel-The Prizes," *Wikipedia*, accessed January 1, 2011, http://en.wikipedia.org/wiki/Alfred_Nobel#The_Prizes.

¹ "The Nobel Peace Prize," Nobelprize.org, accessed February 22, 2011, http://nobelprize.org/nobel_prizes/peace/.

¹ "David Robinson Hall of Fame Speech," YouTube video, 7:45, posted by "mad0214," September 12, 2009, accessed November 25, 2010, http://www.youtube.com/watch?v=yh96tCHVjC4.

¹ "Pouncing scene," *The Lion King*, directed by Roger Allers and Rob Minkoff. (Burbank, CA: Walt Disney Pictures, 1994), DVD.

¹ Spencer Johnson, *The Precious Present* (New York: Knopf Doubleday, 1984), 3.

Bonus chapter The man I know now . . .

¹ "Penny Hardaway," *Wikipedia,* accessed January 21, 2011, http://en.wikipedia.org/wiki/Penny_Hardaway.

¹ Charles Swindoll, *Laugh Again: Experience Outrageous Joy* (Nashville: W Publishing, 1992), 19.

¹ Victor Frankl, *Man's Search for Meaning* (New York: Washington Square Press, 1959), 64.

¹ "The Quote Garden," Terri Guillemets, accessed January 21, 2011, http://www.quotegarden.com/truth.html.

¹ "Ralph Waldo Emerson quotes," ThinkExist, accessed February 17, 2011, http://thinkexist.com/quotation/to_laugh_often_and_much-to_win_the_respect_of/255196.html.

¹ "Experience quotes," ThinkExist, accessed February 17, 2011, http://thinkexist.com/quotations/experience/.

¹ "Listening quotes," ThinkExist, access February 28, 2011, http://thinkexist.com/quotations/listening/.

¹ "What lies behind us quotes," ThinkExist, accessed February 28, 2011, http://thinkexist.com/quotation/what_lies_behind_us_and_what_lies_before_us_are/10712.html.

¹ "Enduring quotes," ThinkExist, accessed March 1, 2011, http://thinkexist.com/quotes/with/keyword/enduring/2.html.

¹ John Maxwell, *Talent Is Never Enough* (Nashville: Thomas Nelson, 2007), 27.

¹ "The Quote Garden," Terri Guillemets, accessed February 28, 2011, http://www.quotegarden.com/kindness.html.

STAY CONNECTED

Thank you for purchasing the Special Edition of The Man I Never Knew: How Leadership Can Be Developed by Faith, Family, and Friends. Dr. Jones wants to hear from you! Below are a few ways you can stay connected. Visit www.drsamueljones.com for more information.

TWITTER @drsjones
Linkedin drsamueljones
FACEBOOK Samuel Jones
INSTAGRAM #Lifechangingpresentations
GOOGLE Samuel Jones

www.ingramcontent.com/pod-product-compliance
Lightning Source LLC
Chambersburg PA
CBHW031956080426
42735CB00007B/411